MISMEASURING OUR LIVES

ALSO BY JOSEPH E. STIGLITZ

Freefall: America, Free Markets, and the Sinking of the World Economy

Globalization and Its Discontents

Making Globalization Work

The Roaring Nineties: A New History of the World's Most Prosperous Decade

The Stiglitz Report: Reforming the International Monetary and Financial Systems in the Wake of the Global Crisis

The Three Trillion Dollar War: The True Cost of the Iraq Conflict (with Linda J. Bilmes)

MISMEASURING OUR LIVES

Why GDP Doesn't Add Up

The Report by the Commission on the
Measurement of Economic Performance
and Social Progress

JOSEPH E. STIGLITZ, AMARTYA SEN,
AND JEAN-PAUL FITOUSSI

THE NEW PRESS

NEW YORK
LONDON

Requests for permission to reproduce selections from this book should be mailed to:
Permissions Department, The New Press, 38 Greene Street, New York, NY 10013

Published in the United States by The New Press, New York, 2010
Distributed by Perseus Distribution

LIBRARY OF CONGRESS CATALOGING-IN-PUBLICATION DATA

Commission on the Measurement of Economic Performance and Social
Progress (France)
Mismeasuring our lives : why GDP doesn't add up / the report by the
Commission on the Measurement of Economic Performance and Social
Progress ; Joseph E. Stiglitz, Amartya Sen, and Jean-Paul Fitoussi.
    p.   cm.
Includes bibliographical references.
ISBN 978-1-59558-519-6 (pb)
1. Economic indicators.   2. Gross domestic product.   3. Social
indicators.   4. Quality of life.   I. Stiglitz, Joseph E.   II. Sen, Amartya,
1933–   III. Fitoussi, Jean-Paul.   IV. Title.
HB137.C655 2010
339.3'1—dc22

2009046692

The New Press was established in 1990 as a not-for-profit alternative to the large,
commercial publishing houses currently dominating the book publishing industry.
The New Press operates in the public interest rather than for private gain, and is
committed to publishing, in innovative ways, works of educational, cultural, and
community value that are often deemed insufficiently profitable.

www.thenewpress.com

Composition by Westchester Book Group

Printed in the United States of America

2   4   6   8   10   9   7   5   3   1

CONTENTS

OTHER MEMBERS OF THE COMMISSION ON THE MEASUREMENT OF ECONOMIC PERFORMANCE AND SOCIAL PROGRESS AND RAPPORTEURS

Other Members

Bina Agarwal	*University of Delhi*
Anthony B. Atkinson	*Nuffield College*
François Bourguignon	*Paris School of Economics*
Jean-Philippe Cotis	*INSEE*
Angus S. Deaton	*Princeton University*
Kemal Dervis	*UNPD*
Marc Fleurbaey	*Université Paris 5*
Nancy Folbre	*University of Massachussetts*
Jean Gadrey	*Université Lille*
Enrico Giovannini	*OECD*
Roger Guesnerie	*Collège de France*
James J. Heckman	*Chicago University*
Geoffrey Heal	*Columbia University*
Claude Henry	*Sciences-Po/Columbia University*
Daniel Kahneman	*Princeton University*
Alan B. Krueger	*Princeton University*
Andrew J. Oswald	*University of Warwick*
Robert D. Putnam	*Harvard University*
Nick Stern	*London School of Economics*
Cass Sunstein	*University of Chicago*
Philippe Weil	*Sciences-Po*

Rapporteurs

Jean-Etienne Chapron	*INSEE*
General Rapporteur	
Didier Blanchet	*INSEE*
Jacques Le Cacheux	*OFCE*
Marco Mira D'ercole	*OCDE*
Pierre-Alain Pionnier	*INSEE*
Laurence Rioux	*INSEE/CREST*
Paul Schreyer	*OCDE*
Xavier Timbeau	*OFCE*
Vincent Marcus	*INSEE*

FOREWORD

I hold a firm belief: We will not change our behavior unless we change the ways we measure our economic performance.

If we do not want our future and the future of our children and grandchildren to be riddled with financial, economic, social, and environmental disasters, which are ultimately human disasters, we must change the way we live, consume, and produce. We must change the criteria governing our social organizations and our public policies.

A tremendous revolution awaits us—we can all feel it.

This revolution will only be fully completed if it is first of all a revolution in our minds, in the way we think, in our mind-sets and values.

Such a revolution is inconceivable without deeply challenging the way we represent the consequences of what we undertake, the results of what we do.

If we apply the critical approach proposed by the commission headed by Joseph Stiglitz to the past two or three decades, and this leads us to revise our judgment regarding the consequences of our choices; if our models ultimately prove to have been counter-models; if our performance ultimately proves to have been poor—then the need for change becomes compellingly obvious.

But if we remain convinced that we have made genuine, sustainable progress during these years, why change?

Our statistics and accounts reflect our aspirations, the values that we assign things. They are inseparable from our vision of the world and the economy, of society, and our conception of human beings and our interrelations. Treating these as objective data, as if they are external to us, beyond question or dispute, is undoubtedly reassuring and comfortable, but it's dangerous. It is dangerous because we get to the point where we stop asking ourselves about the purpose of what we are doing, what we are actually measuring, and what lessons we need to draw.

That is how the mind begins to close, leaving a doctrinaire approach with no room for doubt.

That is how we begin to march ahead blindly while convinced that we know where we're going.

That is how we begin to create a gulf of incomprehension between the expert certain in his knowledge and the citizen whose experience of life is completely out of synch with the story told by the data. This gulf is dangerous because the citizens end up believing that they are being deceived. Nothing is more destructive of democracy.

All over the world, people believe that they are being lied to, that the figures are false, that they are being manipulated. . . . And there are good reasons for their feeling this way. For years, people whose lives were becoming more and more difficult were told that their living standards were rising. How could they not feel deceived?

For years, people were told that finance is a powerful engine of growth, only to discover one day that the risk it had accumulated was so great that it had plunged the world into chaos. Who could fail to understand why those who had lost their home, their job, their pension, would feel deceived?

For years the statistics portrayed increasingly strong economic growth as a victory over scarcity, until it came to light that this growth was endangering the future of the planet and was destroying more than it was creating. Is it any wonder that those whom we are now asking to make efforts and sacrifices and change their way of life before it is too late feel deceived?

The point is not that anyone wished to deceive people deliberately, for neither the statisticians defending the relevance of their GDP or price index nor the accountants convinced that their "fair value" is the best possible measure of an asset's worth are liars.

The problem stems from the fact that our world, our society, and our economy have changed, and the measures have not kept pace. The problem stems from the fact that ultimately, without even realizing it, the statistics and the accounts were made to say things that they weren't saying and that they couldn't say. We have wound up mistaking our representations of wealth for the wealth itself, and our representations of reality for the reality itself. But reality always ends up having the last word.

It is possible to go for a long time without paying the true price of scarcity and risk while being convinced of the contrary, but sooner or later the true price has to be paid. The bill is then much heavier, as behaviors based on these erroneous economic calculations have heightened the scarcity and the risk.

This is the situation in which we find ourselves today.

We have built a cult of the data, and we are now enclosed within. The enormous consequences of what we have done are beginning to dawn on us.

With all this in mind, in February 2008 I asked Joseph Stiglitz, Amartya Sen, and Jean-Paul Fitoussi to set up a commission composed of the world's leading experts. To remedy the situation we face, we had to break with the old ways of thinking. A debate had to be launched at last. It had to be carried on at the highest levels of expertise. And it had to be global.

This was the spirit in which the members of the commission were selected and carried out their work. They devoted their time, their intelligence, and their knowledge to this mission. What they accomplished in eighteen months is remarkable. A collective discussion has now been launched at the international level. And it will go on and on.

I would like to pay special tribute to Joseph Stiglitz, Amartya Sen, and Jean-Paul Fitoussi. Without them, nothing would have been possible. It is thanks to their prestige, their authority, and their energy that so much expertise could be brought together.

There will be a "before" this commission, and an "after."

There will be a "before" this report, and an "after."

Events have ensured that this report is arriving at a decisive moment. The crisis is not only giving us the freedom to imagine other models, another future, and another world—it compels us to do so.

It would have been impossible to launch this debate in a world of certainties, convinced that it was heading in the right direction. At best the report would have been confined to academia. The experts would have discussed it. There would have been a decision to change a few indices. Perhaps there would have been progress on a few specifics. But there would have been no change in the way things were measured and the data were viewed. We could not have compelled a debate about our collective representations and about the purposes of what we are doing.

This shows that, in today's circumstances, this report is important not just technically. It is also important politically. It deals with questions that concern not only economists, statisticians, and accountants, but also politics.

France will put debate on this report's conclusions on the agenda of every international gathering and of every meeting and discussion concerned with the construction of a new global economic, social, and environmental order. France will strive to get all the international organizations to modify their statistical systems in accordance with the commission's recommendations. It will propose to its European partners that Europe set an example by implementing the recommendations. France will adapt its own statistical system accordingly, and it will put the study of this report on the curriculum of all the country's civil service training institutions.

If, at some point or other during their training, everyone in the world in a position of responsibility were to study this report's contents and establish a minimum critical distance from the dominant statistical and accounting model, decisions would no longer be taken as they are today, and the world would find itself radically changed.

We do not have the time to wait for the slow shifting of mind-sets and the gradual awakening of a growing number of leaders, scientists, and experts to one day produce results.

In February 2008, I felt the urgent need to do away with the set ideas and dogmas that had locked in all our thinking and action, and that were making us lie to ourselves. I felt the urgent need to stop giving the response to all those voicing their troubles, difficulties, suffering, doubts, and anxieties: "You are wrong: our statistics prove the contrary." I felt the urgent need to eliminate this dialogue of the deaf that was undermining democracy.

In the comments on the commission's work that Joseph Stiglitz, Amartya Sen, and Jean-Paul Fitoussi sent me, I noted this sentence: "One of the reasons that most people may perceive themselves as being worse off even though average GDP is increasing is *because they are indeed worse off.*" The fact that some of our most prestigious economists are saying this so frankly was absolutely indispensable in order for us to get things clear in our own minds, to put the public debate back on a foundation of truth, and to change our relationship with the truth. There has indeed been a long-standing problem with what we calculate and the way we use what we find. The experts have been aware of this for a long time, and they've been discussing it for a long time. But this discussion didn't change anything. It made no impact. We knew that our indicators had limitations, but we went on using them as if they didn't. They made communications easier. Above all, these indicators were a key component of our vision of the economy and society and of an ideology that had spread all over the world; calling them into question seemed so outrageous that no one would even seriously consider it. We preferred to wait for the contradictions and blind alleys to emerge on their own. That day has come. But, as we all know, victory is far from a foregone conclusion.

The intellectual, moral, and political battle has begun between those who want everything to go back to the way things were before, because they are unable to change the way they think or out of self-interest, and those who are convinced that nothing can stay the same as before and that change must be made as quickly as possible.

France has chosen its camp. It will be a force for proposals and change. All those who play a role in the conduct of world affairs have a historic responsibility.

The world tomorrow will no longer be the same as before the crisis, as breaches have been made in fixed mind-sets and can no longer be closed.

The world tomorrow will no longer be the same because everywhere mentalities are changing and will continue to do so.

There are injustices, improprieties, acts of folly that in future will no longer be tolerable and will not be tolerated.

It remains to be seen whether we will be capable of making this change in a relatively quick and cooperative way, guided by common sense, or whether we will await new disasters to impose change on us that we are incapable of deciding upon ourselves.

We are in a period of history when politicians cannot content themselves with being managers, with simply sorting out the present economic situation and assisting with change.

They must instigate the change, accelerate it, and determine its objectives. Politics is the collective project, the human will pitted against all types of determinism and fatalism. It is the freedom that we all have to choose our destiny together.

The situation is urgent.

We are in one of those eras when, with our certainties shattered and our traditional ways of thinking shown to be impotent, everything has to be rebuilt and reinvented. We are in an era when the central question for politics is what model of development, what model of society and civilization, we aspire to live under and bequeath to our children.

After so many excesses and so many mistakes, and facing such a serious ongoing crisis, when the world has come so close to the abyss, the question of devising a "politics of civilization" is not detached from reality, a matter for consideration in some distant future that is irrelevant to the difficulties of the present. It is a question for today that calls for an immediate answer because the time to change our trajectory is now. Amidst all these difficulties we cannot rest content with reacting on a day-to-day basis; we will not recover from the crisis with just ad hoc solutions.

We have to know where we want to go and what goals we are pursuing.

When the commission ponders the relationship between quantity and quality, between the objective and the subjective, and between the market and the nonmarket sectors, it is clearly reflecting on the conception we have of what we call civilization, the basis on which we are going to judge what we accomplish.

If we refer to a representation of the world in which the services people render within a family have no value compared with those we can obtain on the market, we are expressing an idea of civilization in which the family no longer counts for much. Who could imagine that this won't have consequences?

If leisure has no accounting value because it is essentially filled with nonmarket activities such as sports and culture, this means that we are putting the criterion of high productivity above that of the realization of human potential, contrary to the humanist values that we proclaim. Who could imagine that this won't have consequences?

If the poor maintenance of transport infrastructures causes more accidents and higher repair costs, and even higher medical costs, which increase output; if we count activities that lengthen the distance between home and work and increase insecurity and exclusion as positive contributions to progress; if ever-growing nervous tension, stress, and anxiety undermine society, and the ever-greater resources devoted to fighting their effects are included in economic growth—if we do all this, then what, concretely, is left of our notion of progress?

If we give no value in our accounts to the quality of public service; if we remain locked into an index of economic progress that includes only what is created and not what is destroyed; if we look only at gross domestic production, which rises when there has been an earthquake, a fire, or an environmental disaster; if we don't deduct from what we produce what we consume in the course of production; if we don't include the drafts that we are drawing on the future; if we don't take account of how innovation is accelerating capital depreciation—how can we expect to realize what we are really doing and face up to our responsibilities?

The kind of civilization we build depends on the way we do our accounts quite simply because it changes the value we put on things. And I'm not speaking just about market value.

Our measuring systems make financial trading a high added-value activity. But it is set up only to manage a risk that has been deliberately created and that it is contributing to increasing. If financial trading creates the volatility it claims to protect against, where is the value to society of the service rendered?

If our measuring systems overvalue the usefulness to society of speculation compared with work, entrepreneurship, and creative intelligence, then this dangerously reverses the value system underpinning our vision of progress and introduces into the heart of capitalism a contradiction that can only end up ruining it.

Our measuring systems make us reason on the basis of averages. But if we go on reasoning in averages, we will forge our beliefs and build our decisions on data that are increasingly divorced from real life. The average individual doesn't exist, and heightening inequality is detaching this average even more from the real experience of life, for talking about the average is a way to avoid talking about inequality.

Behind the cult of the data, behind all our statistical and accounting representations, there lies the cult of the market, which is always right. There is this idea that the market can resolve all problems and assign everything a true price.

If the market had the answer to everything, we'd know, and if it were never wrong, it would be obvious.

There are incomplete markets, and there are imperfect markets.

The market does not give us a sense of meaning, or responsibilities, or projects, or vision—and the financial markets even less so.

We don't know the value of an asset because the market prices it every second. The truth is quite the opposite.

The law of supply and demand has to be able to find expression.

The market gives us valuable information. But a project for society or for civilization cannot be built based solely on the market. A project for civilization is born out of a collective will, a collective effort over the long term. It is not the fruit of the instantaneous confrontation of supply and demand.

We will not resolve the problem of global warming simply by allowing a supply–demand balance to be established on the carbon market, any more than we have managed to control economic and financial risks by allowing a balance to be established on the venture markets.

We cannot focus solely on the data the market supplies us. By acting as though the market were the source of all truth, you wind up believing it. But if that belief were true, we wouldn't be where we are. Markets and statistics are being made to say things that they are incapable of saying.

I firmly believe that from now on this will no longer be possible.

This report doesn't tell us where the truth lies, but it does tell us how to look for it. It compels everyone to face up to their responsibilities, to reason differently, and to decide differently. This report does not replace one single statistical approach by another—and this is what makes it so rich and meaningful. It shatters the very idea of a doctrinaire approach. It releases us from this tragic belief we've been locked into whereby there's nothing more to decide since there is only one way of seeing things.

This report frees our minds.

It's now or never.

The only thing that will save us is unchaining our minds so as to gather the strength to make the necessary changes.

The only thing that will save us is unchaining our minds so as to free ourselves from conformism, conservatism, and short-sighted interests.

Let there be no doubt that this report contributes to that effort.

—Nicolas Sarkozy

PREFACE

In an increasingly performance-oriented society, metrics matter. What we measure affects what we do. If we have the wrong metrics, we will strive for the wrong things. In the quest to increase GDP, we may end up with a society in which citizens are worse off.

Too often, we confuse ends with means. One of the criticisms of our economies in the years prior to the crisis is that they did exactly that—a financial sector is a means to a more productive economy, not an end in itself. It is even worse to confuse an improvement in a measurement of well-being with an improvement in well-being itself. Our economy is supposed to increase our well-being. It too is not an end in itself.

The objective of this international Commission was to align better the metrics of well-being with what actually contributes to quality of life, and in doing so, to help all of us to direct efforts to those things that really matter.

The Commission was appointed by Nicholas Sarkozy, President of the Republic of France, in early 2008 in response to increasing concerns about the adequacy of current measures of economic performance, in particular those based on GDP figures, and to broader concerns about the relevance of these figures as measures of societal well-being, as well as measures of economic, environmental and social sustainability.

The Commission was charged with looking at the entire range of issues, and was given full independence in the conduct of its work. The Commission consisted of an international panel of experts, chosen for their expertise in one or another area of enquiry. Its aim was to identify the limits of GDP as an indicator of economic performance and social progress, to consider additional information required for the production of a more relevant picture, to discuss how to present this information in the most appropriate way and to assess the feasibility of alternative measurement tools. The Commission's work was not focused on France, or on developed countries. It was hoped that the output of the Commission would provide a template for every interested country or group of countries, and would spur further work and discussion on these issues around the world.

The Commission was chaired by Professor Joseph E. Stiglitz, Columbia University. Professor Amartya Sen, Harvard University, served as Chair Adviser. Professor Jean-Paul Fitoussi, Institut d'Etudes Politiques de Paris, President of the Observatoire Français des Conjonctures Economiques (OFCE), was Coordinator of the Commission. Members of the Commission are renowned experts from universities, governmental and intergovernmental organizations in several countries (United States, France, United Kingdom, India). Rapporteurs and secretariats are provided by the French national statistical institute (Insee), OFCE and OECD. The full list of commissioners is provided on p. vii.

The final report of the Commission was publicly presented on September 14, 2009, in a discussion led by President Sarkozy, with contributions from members of the panel and comments from heads of international organizations and French ministers: Angel Gurria, Secretary General of the OECD; Juan Somavia, director general of the International Labour Office; Jacques Barrot, Vice-President of the European Commission; Christine Lagarde, Minister for Economic Affairs, Industry and Employment; Chantal Jouanno, Secretary of State, Minister of Ecology, Energy, Sustainable Development and Sea, in charge of Green Technologies and of Climate Change Negotiations. The IMF and the World Bank were also represented at a high level.

National Income Accounting Goes from the Province of Technicians to a Subject of Public Discourse

It is easy to understand why suddenly a set of issues that have been the province of technicians have become a source of public policy debate. Trying to understand what makes for good performance of a society is central to the social sciences. We see the world through lenses not only shaped by our ideologies and ideas but also shaped by the statistics we use to measure what is going on, the latter being frequently linked to the former. GDP per capita is the commonly used metric; governments are pleased when they can report that GDP per capita has arisen, say, by 5%. But other numbers can tell a very different picture. In Russia, declining life expectancy suggests there are underlying problems, even if GDP per capita is rising. So, too, in the United States, most individuals saw a decline in income, adjusted for inflation, from 1999 through 2008—even though GDP per capita was going up—providing a markedly different picture of performance. Such a disparity may arise when income inequality increases at the same time that income increases.

Metrics Shape Our Beliefs and Inferences

The theories we construct, the hypotheses we test and the beliefs we have are all shaped by our systems of metrics. Social scientists often blithely use easily accessible numbers, like GDP, as a basis of their empirical models, without enquiring sufficiently into the limitations and biases in the metrics. Flawed or biased statistics can lead us to make incorrect inferences. In the years preceding the crisis, many in Europe, focusing on higher GDP growth rates, suggested that they should follow the American model. Had they focused on other metrics (such as median income) or if they had made appropriate corrections for the increased indebtedness of American households and the country as a whole—with the consequent risk of non-sustainability—their enthusiasm might have been more muted.

Inevitably, economists attempt to draw inferences about the desirability of policies by making comparisons over time or between countries, and if the metrics employed are imperfect, there is a risk of biased, distorted and flawed inferences. We worry that if there are systematic measurement errors in, say, the output of the public sector, inferences made about the consequences of a large public sector on overall economic performance may be biased, simply because the larger the sector, the more the distortion. Most of the vast amount of empirical work making such "cross-country" comparisons is insufficiently sensitive to these limitations.

Metrics and Policy

For a political leader, these are matters that are not just academic. Flawed inferences affect economic policy. Metrics that give short shrift to the environment (to air, water or noise pollution) put insufficient weight on something that is of vital and increasing importance to many citizens. A political leader ignores these concerns at his peril.

A political leader attempting to fulfill the wishes of his citizens and promote their well-being is pulled in different directions: he will be graded on economic performance, even though much of that is out of his control. But citizens also care about many dimensions of the quality of life—including the quality of the environment. Current metrics suggest that there may be trade-offs—one can improve the environment only by sacrificing a growth measure. But if we had a comprehensive measure of well-being, perhaps we would see this as a false choice: it could indicate an increase in well-being if we improve the environment, even if conventionally measured output went down.

And it is for the same reason that the work of the Commission has drawn such interest from civil society.

Statistics and Information Theory

There is hardly a decision in modern life that is not colored by our statistics and accounting frameworks. The focus of Stiglitz's research over many years was on how information affects economic and political decisions. Our statistical and accounting systems provide, as we have noted, an important part of the framework through which we see and analyze the world. They are critical parts of our "information" systems.

Metrics that seem out of synch with individuals' perceptions are particularly problematic. If GDP is increasing, but most people feel they are worse off, they may worry that governments are manipulating the statistics, in the hope that by telling them that they are better off, they will feel better off. In these cases, confidence in government is eroded, and with the erosion of this confidence, the ability of government to address issues of vital public importance is weakened.

While these public policy concerns were part of the impetus for the work of the Commission, the commissioners decided early on in their work to limit themselves to a focus on our statistical system itself, and not to extend their work to the policy implications that might follow from having a better statistical system. In some cases, these policy implications are obvious, and it would have been easy to achieve consensus among the commissioners. In other cases, reasonable people may come to different policy stances.

On these issues of the reform of our statistical system, what was remarkable was the degree of unanimity among the members of the Commission.

Why Reconsider Metrics Now?

Many of the problems with GDP statistics have been well known. But several factors gave the efforts of our Commission particular relevance. There have been changes in our society and in the structure of our economy that make some of the limitations of GDP accounting of more concern. We mentioned one already: if there is increasing inequality, as there are in many, if not most, countries around the world, there may be an increasing disparity between average income and median income (the income of the representative individual); one may be increasing while the other is declining.

The problems of measurement of government services that are not sold on the market are well known, but these problems become of increasing importance as the share of government expenditures in OECD countries (on average) increases, as it has from about 25% to more than 45% in the last 50 years.

It is obviously more difficult to assess the quantitative importance of quality improvements than to count the quantitative increases in, say, the number of cars; but such quality improvements are of increasing importance. If every family has a car, increased consumption of "automobile services" will take the form of better cars, not more cars. But then we have to have ways to measure these quality differences. This is especially difficult when we have to measure the growth of services.

Globalization itself has meant that the difference between the well-being of the citizens within a country may differ markedly from the output produced within a country. Ironically, the measure focusing on the former, GNP, grew out of fashion, giving way to GDP, which focuses on production, just as globalization was making the difference more important. There are obvious political consequences to the distinction.

When problems of globalization and environmental and resource sustainability are combined, GDP metrics may be especially misleading. A developing country that sells a polluting mining concession with low royalties and inadequate environmental regulation may see GDP increase but well-being decrease.

There are concerns too that a focus on the material aspects of GDP may be especially inappropriate as the world faces the crisis of global warming. Should we "punish" a country—in terms of our measure of performance—if it decides to take some of the fruits of the increase in productivity from the advancement of knowledge in the form of leisure, rather than just consuming more and more goods?

The Crisis as an Opportune Moment

There are several reasons that the timing of President Sarkozy's initiative was particularly opportune. One was the crisis that overcame the world just as our work began.

The Commission was established before the recession hit; and the scientific work of the Commission, reflecting ongoing research on the underlying problems of the measurement of economic performance and social progress, was not affected by the crisis. But, especially for some members of the Commission, the crisis heightened the importance and relevance of the Commission's work and underscored certain problems with which it had been grappling. Even before the crisis, Commission members had expressed a belief that a good set of metrics capture the notion of economic and environmental sustainability. It was clear that GDP by itself did not do this. Similarly, before the crisis, Commission members had expressed a concern about the appropriate use of market prices, especially for evaluating long-run sustainability. The crisis has illustrated the importance of both of these concerns. The seemingly strong performance of some countries prior to the crisis (as indicated by GDP) was not sustainable and was based on "bubble" prices that exaggerated profits and output.

Advances in Research

While changes in our economies and societies, including those to which we alluded earlier, have resulted in a sense that the old metrics may be increasingly deficient, especially as measures of well-being, advances in research across a number of disciplines enables us now to develop broader, more encompassing measures of well-being. Some of these dimensions are reflected in traditional statistics but are given more prominence: unemployment has an effect on well-being that goes well beyond the loss of income to which it gives rise.

The timing of the Commission was opportune for another reason. Criticisms of the traditional measures were being expressed in many quarters, including by civil society. Changes in the structure of our economy raised questions about whether some of the assumptions made in the past were still appropriate. Global warming had put issues of sustainability front and center.

For some of these, there may be objective metrics, but for others, replicable subjective assessments may provide the best approach to measurement. Individuals may, for instance, be affected by their sense of security and by their bonds with others. But even the seemingly noneconomic factors are affected by economic structures. Reforms in the workplace may lead to increased market efficiency but lower worker job satisfaction and therefore a reduction in their sense of well-being. Some economic reforms in recent years may have increased GDP but may have had adverse effects on important dimensions of quality of life. For instance, one of the criticisms of globalization (in the way it has proceeded) is that it has contributed to the weakening of a sense of community, thereby leading to a decrease in a sense of well-being. It is important to have metrics that would allow us to assess such claims.

This work is just at its beginning stage, and yet the results obtained so far are extremely promising. It has been clearly established that replicable measurement of many of those factors affecting well-being and the quality of life is possible.

A Single Metric or a Dashboard?

The purposes of our statistical systems are multiple, and a metric that is designed for one purpose may be ill-suited to another.

Changing Objectives

National income statistics like GDP and GNP were originally introduced to provide a measure of the level of market-based economic activity (including the public sector but excluding home production). Especially after the development of Keynesian economics and in the aftermath of the Great Depression, as governments took on the responsibility of managing the economy, it became important for them to have statistics that described the state of the economy. To manage an economy without indicators of how well the economy was doing has been described like trying to fly an airplane without instruments.

Two of the pioneers in this work, Simon Kuznets and Richard Stone, both received the Nobel Prize, in part for their contributions in creating systems of national income accounts.

Much of the work of national income statisticians in subsequent years has been directed at correcting imperfections in the measure of market activity (for instance, the valuation of housing services or government activity). Some of the work of national income statisticians has been directed at expanding the scope of economic activity, to include, for instance, home production.

But these metrics have increasingly been thought of as measures of societal well-being. Of course, good national income statisticians have warned against these abuses, even as they have worked hard to make our measures better reflect the real level of economic activity and increasingly focused on measures, say, of the real income of households.

Much economic activity occurs within the home—and this can contribute to individual well-being as much or more than market production. A shift in the locus of production may not necessarily be indicative of an improvement in well-being.

Still, this work has centered on attempting to *adapt* market measures so that they better reflect societal well-being. Today, there is a growing demand for more encompassing measures of social progress and societal well-being, which, while incorporating metrics of market activity, are not limited to such metrics. One contribution of the Commission was to provide further impetus to these attempts.

The Need for Multiple Metrics

There is no single indicator that can capture something as complex as our society. Trying to capture what is going on by using a set of numbers that is too small can be grossly misleading. We might want to know how fast we are driving (55 miles an hour) and how far we can go before we run out of gasoline (250 miles), but a single metric, say formed by adding the two numbers (305) would tell us nothing about either question.

We care about how we are doing "in the aggregate," but we also care about what is happening to the distribution of income. We care, moreover, not just for how well-off we are today, but for how well-off we will be in the future. If we are borrowing from the future, we at least want to know that our current level of well-being is not sustainable. While there are many dimensions of sustainability, environmental sustainability has taken on increasing importance, especially with the realization that, with global warming, the world is currently on an unsustainable path.

The goal, then, is to construct a simple set of metrics that captures much that is of central concern. That is why we should expect that a revised GDP measure will continue to be used as a measure of market activity; but it will be supplemented by measures that reflect more broadly what is happening to most citizens (measures of median income), what is happening to the poor (measures of poverty), what is happening to the environment (measurements of resource depletion and environmental degradation) and what is happening to economic sustainability (measurements of debt).

Global Resonance and Global and National Dialogues

The concerns raised by President Sarkozy and our Commission have, not surprisingly, struck a global chord. There is resonance throughout the world. Even before the work of the Commission, Bhutan was hard at work creating a measure of GNH, Gross National Happiness, and Thailand was working on its own index.

Because what we choose to measure and how we construct our measures can have such an important role in the decisions that are made, it is important that there be an open and public discussion of our system of metrics.

Hopefully, this report will play a role in this public dialogue. Indeed, we believe that our report may stimulate such a dialogue, as countries come to analyze what is important to them, and whether their systems of metric adequately capture these values. The vitality of the discourse that is already occurring is exemplified by the Third OECD World Forum on "Statistics, Knowledge, and Policy," held in Busan, Korea, on October 27–30, 2009, where participants considered how better ways of measuring the progress of societies could play an important role not only in charting progress but also in "building visions" and "improving life."

Unfinished Business

We view our study as neither the beginning nor the end of a journey. The Commission was fortunate to be able to draw from a large body of work on the issues with which we were concerned. The early developers of GDP metrics were clearly far more aware of the assumptions that went into the construction of the index than many of those who have subsequently found the measure of such use. But by reminding modern-day researchers of the limitations and biases in existing measures, we hope that some of our analyses will not only lead to better metrics but will also unleash a flood of studies to help us understand the sensitivity of, for instance, the inferences of the metrics used.

We devoted considerable efforts to thinking about what kinds of reforms in our metrics might lead to better indicators. But often the data required is not available. Thus, much of our report is devoted to recommendations for future work, including that by statistical agencies in gathering data.

This is just the first step in what should be an ongoing effort. Even if we had succeeded in constructing the perfect measure for today, changes in our economy and our society would necessitate constantly revisiting these issues. But we are far from that goal.

The effort to improve our statistics also needs to be a global effort, one in which political leadership is necessary if we are to obtain the requisite momentum. That was one of the reasons that so many of the commissioners, who had devoted so much of their professional lives to these issues, were so enthusiastic about this initiative: President Sarkozy was providing the political impetus.

The reception to our report of September 2009 has been heartening—and reinforced our conviction of the importance of the issues raised by the Commission. Our hope was that the work of the Commission would lead to a broad dialogue on societal objectives, whether commonly used metrics were consistent with those objectives, and whether there were alternatives that would be more consonant with broadly held values.

The timing of our report was, in this sense, fortunate. It coincided with broader skepticism by many citizens about the direction in which society was going. Global warming had become a paramount concern in many parts of the world, and yet no account had been taken of the adverse effects of the increase in materialistic consumption—seemingly "lauded" by GDP measures—and whether the planet could survive this increase.

At the launch of our report in Paris on September 14, 2009, both President Sarkozy and Angel Gurria, the Secretary General of the OECD, committed to carrying forward the work of the commission. At the Third International Knowledge Forum, the work of the Commission helped shape discussions of new approaches to assessing well-being. A number of countries have begun work implementing the ideas of the Commission. And President Sarkozy carried the discussion of these issues to the G-20 meeting in Pittsburgh shortly thereafter.

Personal Notes

As we noted, many members of the Commission had been involved in these and similar issues for much of their professional lives. They have been advocating reforms in our statistical systems and doing the research on the basis of which such reforms could be made.

Amartya Sen had worked, along with Mahbub ul Haq, in the establishment of the Human Development approach of the United Nations, with systematic presentation of information related to the well-being and freedom of people—of which the Human Development Index (the well-known HDI) is the simplest representation. The HDI showed that the ranking of countries using a broader metric, which included health and education, could be markedly different from that focusing just on income. The capabilities approach that Sen had previously developed was very influential in the thinking of the members of the Commission.

We noted earlier that accounting frameworks, at both the corporate and national levels, are an essential part of our information systems. Stiglitz has long been concerned (both in his theoretical work, and in his work as Chairman of President Clinton's Council of Economic Advisers and Chief Economist of the World Bank) about how we could improve these accounting frameworks and enhance the quality of the information that forms the bases of decision making in our economic and political systems. Some of our proposed reforms were far less ambitious than those proposed here—simply a better accounting of resource depletion and environmental degradation. And yet, political resistance was so great that these initiatives were thwarted. It showed the power of information. There were those who were afraid of the light that better information systems might shed. That key interest groups did not want this kind of information to be publicly disseminated suggested these reforms in our statistical system might have real impacts.

As chief economist of the World Bank, Stiglitz was particularly concerned about how judgments about impacts on GDP could lead to wrong decisions about resource development. Many developing countries were being urged to privatize natural resource extraction, even if meant that much of the profits went abroad. GDP would be increased by the mining activity. But when account was taken of the fact that the profits accrued to those abroad, GNP might not increase. And when further account was taken of the depletion of resources and adverse effects on health and environment, it was even clearer that the citizens of the country might be worse off.

The focus of Fitoussi's research over many years was to show how changes in the distribution of micro-economic variables affected not only the perception of macro-economic variables but also the conclusions of macro-economic models. Inequality is of the essence, and not taking it appropriately into consideration may lead to the wrong inferences about macro-economic policies.

For so many of the members of the Commission, then, the opportunity to work on this Commission was a chance to push an agenda with which they had long been associated, to give it momentum on a global scale.

This Volume

Though the work of the Commission was written largely by and for social scientists (mostly economists, but the Commission included a prominent political scientist, a prominent sociologist and a prominent economic psychologist), we wanted to reach out more broadly. As we noted, we were interested not just in better metrics, but in using a discussion of metrics to engage a broader dialogue about societal values and objectives. The chapters contained in this book represent the nontechnical report of the Commission; the technical chapters are available at the web site of the Commission: www.stiglitz-sen-fitoussi.fr. But to set the context for the issues under discussion, we begin the volume with a broad overview, written by Fitoussi, Sen and Stiglitz.

The subject of our inquiry was so broad and complex that, in the initial meeting of the Commission, it was decided to divide the work among three working groups. One would focus on the standard but difficult issues of national income accounting: measurement of output of government, adjustments for an open economy, treatment of household production and leisure and "defensive" expenditures—expenditures required just to maintain the status quo, for example, through maintaining security. The second focused on efforts to measure "quality of life," the sense of well-being. And the third focused on sustainability. Global warming had brought the issue of environmental sustainability front and center; the global financial and economic crisis had raised similar questions for economic sustainability. A cross-cutting focus, affecting the work of all the working groups, concerned distributional issues—how to capture appropriately the diverse situations confronting different individuals. Most of the statistical indicators focus on averages; but when inequality is changing, what happens at the bottom, or even the middle, can differ markedly from what is happening, say, to per-capita GDP.

The initial meeting of the Commission was held in Paris, in April 2009. Subsequent plenary meetings of the Commission and of the working groups were held in New York and in Paris. Preliminary versions of the Report by the Commission were posted on the internet site. Many of the suggestions by commentators are reflected in the final draft of the Commission report.

Acknowledgments

We could not have accomplished what we did were it not for the vast amount of work on the subject that had been done by national income scholars and statisticians over an extended period of time, only some of which could be acknowledged in the individual chapters.

In the years after Kuznets's and Stone's pioneering work, vast amounts of work have been done on many of the areas under discussion here: the measurement of output in the public sector or inside the household, the measurement of resource depletion and environmental degradation, the particular problems that arise in "open economies," dealing with the consequences of inequality or ascertaining sustainability and measuring "happiness."

We need to recognize the important work of the OECD, not only in helping to give prominence to the issues at hand and for their technical contributions to the subject but also for the support they gave to the work of the Commission, including through Enrico Giovanni, the OECD's former chief statistician, who spearheaded their efforts in this arena and served as chair on one of the Commission's three working groups.

We conclude with a word of acknowledgment to all of those whose contributions played such a role in the work of the Commission. We first want to thank the President of the French Republic, Nicholas

Sarkozy, for convening the Commission, for the support he has given us, and for the complete freedom he has provided us in the conduct of our work. We also want to thank the other commissioners for the enormous amount of effort they put into the work of the Commission and for their sense of commitment and purpose, which allowed the resolution of even quite disparate positions. Given this hard work, we hesitate to single out any commissioners for attention, but we feel we would be remiss if we did not acknowledge those who served as chairmen of the three working groups—Enrico Giovanni, Geoff Heal and Alan Krueger, who served, respectively, as chairs of the working groups on problems with "standard" national income statistics, on the measurement of sustainability and on metrics of well-being and quality of life. We need also to acknowledge the work of the rapporteurs, headed by Jean-Etienne Chapron, who took to heart all the comments and suggestions made by the commissioners and managed to produce the final report. Finally, we want to thank the French Ministry of Economic Affairs and the French National Statistical Institute (INSEE) for the logistic and intellectual help they provided during the eighteen months of the functioning of the Commission.

—Joseph E. Stiglitz, Amartya Sen, and Jean-Paul Fitoussi
January 2010

MISMEASURING OUR LIVES

EXECUTIVE SUMMARY

Why Has This Report Been Written?

In February 2008, the President of the French Republic, Nicholas Sarkozy, unsatisfied with the present state of statistical information about the economy and the society, asked Joseph Stiglitz (President of the Commission), Amartya Sen (Advisor) and Jean-Paul Fitoussi (Coordinator) to create a Commission, subsequently called "The Commission on the Measurement of Economic Performance and Social Progress" (CMEPSP). The Commission's aim has been to identify the limits of GDP as an indicator of economic performance and social progress, including the problems with its measurement; to consider what additional information might be required for the production of more relevant indicators of social progress; to assess the feasibility of alternative measurement tools, and to discuss how to present the statistical information in an appropriate way.

In effect, statistical indicators are important for designing and assessing policies aiming at advancing the progress of society, as well as for assessing and influencing the functioning of economic markets. Their role has increased significantly over the last two decades. This reflects improvements in the level of education in the population, increases in the complexity of modern economies and the widespread use of information technology. In the "information society," access to data, including statistical data, is much easier. More and more people look at statistics to be better informed or to make decisions. To respond to the growing demand for information, the supply of statistics has also increased considerably, covering new domains and phenomena.

What we measure affects what we do; and if our measurements are flawed, decisions may be distorted. Choices between promoting GDP and protecting the environment may be false choices, once environmental degradation is appropriately included in our measurement of economic performance. So too, we often draw inferences about what are good policies by looking at what policies have promoted economic growth; but if our metrics of performance are flawed, so too may be the inferences that we draw.

However, there often seems to be a marked distance between standard measures of important socio-economic variables like economic growth, inflation, unemployment, etc. and widespread perceptions. The standard measures may suggest, for instance that there is less inflation or more growth than individuals perceive to be the case, and the gap is so large and so universal that it cannot be explained by reference to money illusion or to human psychology. In some countries, this gap has undermined confidence in official statistics (for example, in France and in the United Kingdom only one third of citizens trust official figures, and these countries are not exceptions), with a clear impact on the way in which public discourse about the conditions of the economy and necessary policies takes place.

There may be several explanations for the gap between the statistical measurement of socio-economic phenomena and citizen perception of the same phenomena:

- The statistical *concepts* may be correct, but the measurement process may be imperfect.
- In many cases, there are debates about what are the right concepts, and the appropriate use of different concepts.
- When there are large changes in inequality (more generally a change in income distribution) gross domestic product (GDP)

or any other aggregate computed per capita may not provide an accurate assessment of the situation in which most people find themselves. If inequality increases enough relative to the increase in average per capital GDP, most people can be worse off even though average income is increasing.

- The commonly used statistics may not be capturing some phenomena, which have an increasing impact on the wellbeing of citizens. For example, traffic jams may increase GDP as a result of the increased use of gasoline, but obviously not the quality of life. Moreover, if citizens are concerned about the quality of air, and air pollution is increasing, then statistical measures which ignore air pollution will provide an inaccurate estimate of what is happening to citizens' well-being. Or a tendency to measure gradual change may be inadequate to capture risks of abrupt alterations in the environment such as climate change.

- The way in which statistical figures are reported or used may provide a distorted view of the trends of economic phenomena. For example, much emphasis is usually put on GDP although net national product (which takes into account the effect of depreciation), or real household income (which focuses on the real income of households within the economy) may be more relevant. These numbers may differ markedly. Then, GDP is not wrong *as such*, but wrongly used. What is needed is a better understanding of the appropriate use of each measure.

Indeed, for a long time there have been concerns about the adequacy of current measures of economic performance, in particular those solely based on GDP. Besides, there are even broader concerns about the relevance of these figures as measures of societal well-being. To focus specifically on the enhancement of inanimate objects of convenience (for example in the GNP or GDP which have been the focus of a myriad of economic studies of progress), could be ultimately justified—to the extent it could be—only through what these objects do to the human lives they can directly or indirectly influence. Moreover, it has long been clear that GDP is an inadequate metric to gauge well-being over time particularly in its economic, environmental and social dimensions, some aspects of which are often referred to as *sustainability*.

Why Is This Report Important?

Between the time that the Commission began working on this report and the completion of this report, the economic context has radically changed. We are now living one of the worst financial, economic and social crises in post-war history. The reforms in measurement recommended by the Commission would be highly desirable, even if we had not had the crisis. But some members of the Commission believe that the crisis provides heightened urgency to these reforms. They believe that one of the reasons why the crisis took many by surprise is that our measurement system failed us and/or market participants and government officials were not focusing on the right set of statistical indicators. In their view, neither the private nor the public accounting systems were able to deliver an early warning, and did not alert us that the *seemingly* bright growth performance of the world economy between 2004 and 2007 may have been achieved at the expense of future growth. It is also clear that some of the performance was a "mirage," profits that were based on prices that had been inflated by a bubble. It is perhaps going too far to hope that had we had a better measurement system, one that would have signalled problems ahead, so governments might have taken early measures to avoid or at least to mitigate the present turmoil. But perhaps had there been more awareness of the limitations of standard metrics, like GDP, there would have been less euphoria over economic performance in the years prior to the crisis; metrics which incorporated assessments of sustainability (e.g., increasing indebtedness) would have provided a more cautious view of economic performance. But many countries lack a timely and complete set of wealth accounts—the "balance sheets" of the economy—that could give a comprehensive picture of assets, debts and liabilities of the main actors in the economy.

We are also facing a looming environmental crisis, especially associated with global warming. Market prices are distorted by the fact that there is no charge imposed on carbon emissions; and no account is made of the cost of these emissions in standard national income accounts. Clearly, measures of economic performance that reflected these environmental costs might look markedly different from standard measures.

If the view expressed in the preceding paragraphs is not necessarily shared by all members of the Commission, the whole Commission is convinced that the crisis is teaching us a very important lesson: those attempting to guide the economy and our societies are like pilots trying to steering a course without a reliable compass. The decisions they (and we as individual citizens) make depend on what we measure, how good our measurements are and how well our measures are understood. We are almost blind when the metrics on which action is based are ill-designed or when they are not well understood. For many purposes, we need better metrics. Fortunately, research in recent years has enabled us to improve our metrics, and it is time to incorporate in our measurement systems some of these advances. There is also consensus among the Commission members that better measures may enable us to steer our economies better through and out of crises. Many of the indicators put forward by the report will lend themselves to this purpose.

The report is about measurement rather than policies, thus it does not discuss how best our societies could advance through collective actions in the pursuit of various goals. However, as what we measure shapes what we collectively strive to pursue—and what we pursue determines what we measure—the report and its implementation may have a significant impact on the way in which our societies look at themselves and, therefore, on the way in which policies are designed, implemented and assessed.

The Commission notes the important progress in statistical measurement that has occurred in recent years, and urges continued efforts to improve our statistical data base and the indicators that are constructed from this data base. The report indicates avenues for more or different measurement efforts in various domains, and we hope that it will influence future statistical policies in both developed and developing countries, as well as the work of international organizations that play a key role in the development of statistical standards worldwide.

By Whom Has the Report Been Written?

This is a report written by economists and social scientists. The members of the Commission represent a broad range of specializations, from national accounting to the economics of climate change. The members have conducted research on social capital, happiness, and health and mental well-being. They share the belief that it is important to build bridges between different communities—between the producers and users of statistical information, whatever their discipline—that have become increasingly distant in recent years. Commission members see their expertise as a complement to reports on similar topics that were written from a different perspective, for instance by scientists on climate change or by psychologists on mental health. Although the core of the report is rather technical, the summaries of the technical chapter have been written using, as much as possible, non-technical language.

To Whom Is the Report Addressed?

The Commission hopes that the report will find a receptive audience among four distinct groups, and it has been written with that in mind. The report is addressed, first of all, to political leaders. In this time of crises, when new political narratives are necessary to identify where our societies should go, the report advocates a shift of emphasis from a "production-oriented" measurement system to one focused on the well-being of current and future generations, i.e., toward broader measures of social progress.

Second, the report is aimed at reaching policymakers who wish to get a better sense of which indicators are available and useful to design, implement and assess policies aimed at improving well-being and fostering social progress. Policymakers are reminded both of the richness and of the shortcomings of existing data but also of the fact that reliable quantitative information "does not grow on trees" and significant investments need to be made to develop statistics and indicators that provide policymakers with the information they need to make the decisions confronting them.

Third, the report has been written for the academic community, statisticians and intensive users of statistics. They are reminded of how difficult it can be to produce reliable data and of the numerous assumptions that underlay all statistical series. Academics will, hopefully, become more cautious in the confidence they place in certain statistics. Those in national statistical offices will, hopefully find helpful suggestions about areas where further developments might be particularly valuable.

Lastly, the report has been written for civil society organizations that are both users and producers of statistics. More generally, it is addressed to the public at large, whether from richer or poorer countries and whether rich or poor within societies. We hope that through a better understanding of the statistical data and indicators that are available (their strengths and limits), they can make a better assessment of the problems facing their societies. We hope the report will also serve journalists and the media who have a responsibility in enabling citizens to get a sense of what is happening in the society in which they are living. Information is a public good; the more we are informed about what is happening in our society, the better will our democracies be able to function.

What Are the Main Messages and Recommendations?

The report distinguishes between an assessment of *current well-being* and an assessment of *sustainability,* whether this can last over time. Current well-being has to do with both economic resources, such as income, and with non-economic aspects of people's lives (what they do and what they can do, how they feel, and the natural environment they live in). Whether these levels of well-being can be sustained over time depends on whether stocks of capital that matter for our lives (natural, physical, human, social) are passed on to future generations.

To organize its work, the Commission organized itself into three working groups, focusing respectively on: Classical GDP Issues, Quality of Life and Sustainability. The following main messages and recommendations arise from the report.

Towards Better Measures of Economic Performance in a Complex Economy

Before going beyond GDP and tackling the more difficult task of measuring well-being, it is worth asking where existing measures of economic performance need improving. Measuring production—a variable which among other things determines the level of employment—is essential for the monitoring of economic activity. The first main message of our report is that the time has come to adapt our system of measurement of economic activity to better reflect the structural changes which have characterized the evolution of modern economies. In effect, the growing share of services and the production of increasingly complex products make the measurement of output and economic performance more difficult than in the past. There are now many products whose quality is complex, multi-dimensional and subject to rapid change. This is obvious for goods, like cars, computers, washing machines and the like, but is even truer for services, such as medical services, educational services, information and communication technologies, research activities and financial services. In some countries and some sectors, increasing "output" is more a matter of an increase in the quality of goods produced and consumed than in the quantity. Capturing quality change is a tremendous challenge, yet this is vital to measuring real income and real consumption, some of the key determinants of people's material well-being. Underestimating quality improvements is equivalent to overestimating the rate of inflation, and therefore to underestimating real income. The opposite is true when quality improvements are overstated.

Governments play an important part in today's economies. They provide services of a "collective" nature, such as security, and of a more "individual" nature, such as medical services and education. The mix between private and public provision of individual services varies significantly across countries and over time. Beyond the contribution of collective services to citizens' living standards, individual services, particularly education, medical services, public housing or public sports facilities, are almost certainly valued positively by citizens. These services tend to be large in scale, and have increased considerably since World War II, but, in many cases, they remain badly measured. Traditionally, measures have been based on the inputs used to produce these services (such as the number of doctors) rather than on the actual outputs produced (such as the number of particular medical treatments). Making adjustments for quality changes is even more difficult. Because outputs are taken to move in tandem with inputs productivity change in the provision of these services is ignored. It follows that if there is positive (negative) productivity change in the public sector, our measures under (over)-estimate economic growth and real income. For a satisfactory measure of economic performance and living standards it is thus important to come to grips with measuring government output. (In our present, admittedly flawed, system of measurement based on expenditures, government output represents around 20% of GDP in many OECD countries and total government expenditure more than 40% for the OECD countries.)

While there are methodological disagreements about how to make the adjustments to quality or how to go about measuring government output, there is a broad consensus that adjustments should be made, and even about the principles which should guide such adjustments. The disagreements arise in the practical implementation of these principles. In its report the Commission has addressed both the principles and the difficulties in implementations.

From Production to Well-Being

Another key message, and unifying theme of the report, is that the time is ripe for our measurement system to *shift emphasis from measuring economic production to measuring people's well-being.* And measures of well-being should be put in a context of sustainability. Despite deficiencies in our measures of production, we know much more about them than about well-being. Changing emphasis does not mean dismissing GDP and production measures. They emerged from concerns about market production and employment; they continue to provide answers to many important questions such as monitoring economic activity. But emphasizing well-being is important because there appears to be an increasing gap between the information contained in aggregate GDP data and what counts for common people's well-being. This means working towards the development of a statistical system that complements measures of market activity by measures centered on people's well-being and by measures that capture sustainability. Such a system must, of necessity, be plural—because no single measure can summarize something as complex as the well-being of the members of society, our system of measurement must encompass a range of different measures. The issue of aggregation across dimensions (that is to say, how we add up, for example, a measure of health with a measure of consumption of conventional goods), while important, is subordinate to the establishment of a broad statistical system that captures as many of the relevant dimensions as possible. Such a system should not just measure *average* levels of well-being within a given community, and how they change over time, but also document the diversity of people's experiences and the linkages across various dimensions of people's lives. There are several dimensions to well-being but a good place to start is the measurement of material well-being or living standards.

Recommendation 1: When evaluating material well-being, look at income and consumption rather than production.
GDP is the most widely-used measure of economic activity. There are international standards for its calculation, and much thought has gone into its statistical and conceptual bases. Earlier paragraphs have emphasized some of the important areas where more progress is needed in its computation. As statisticians and economists know very well, GDP mainly measures market production—expressed in money units—and as such it is useful. However, it has often been treated as if it were a measure of economic well-being.

Conflating the two can lead to misleading indications about how well-off people are and entail the wrong policy decisions. Material living standards are more closely associated with measures of net national income, real household income and consumption—production can expand while income decreases or vice versa when account is taken of depreciation, income flows into and out of a country, and differences between the prices of output and the prices of consumer products.

Recommendation 2: Emphasize the household perspective.
While it is informative to track the performance of economies as a whole, trends in citizens' material living standards are better followed through measures of household income and consumption. Indeed, the available national accounts data shows that in a number of OECD countries real household income has grown quite differently from real GDP per capita, and typically at a lower rate. The household perspective entails taking account of payments between sectors, such as taxes going to government, social benefits coming from government and interest payments on household loans going to financial corporations. Properly defined, household income and consumption should also reflect in-kind services provided by government, such as subsidized health care and educational services. A major effort of statistical reconciliation will also be required to understand why certain measures such as household income can move differently depending on the underlying statistical source.

Recommendation 3: Consider income and consumption
jointly with wealth.
Income and consumption are crucial for assessing living standards, but in the end they can only be gauged in conjunction with information on wealth. A household that spends its wealth on consumption goods increases its current well-being but at the expense

of its future well-being. The consequences of such behavior would be captured in a household's balance sheet, and the same holds for other sectors of the economy, and for the economy as a whole. To construct balance sheets, we need comprehensive accounts of assets and liabilities. Balance sheets for countries are not novel in concept, but their availability is still limited and their construction should be promoted. Measures of wealth are central to measuring sustainability. What is carried over into the future necessarily has to be expressed as stocks—of physical, natural, human and social capital. The right valuation of these stocks plays a crucial role, and is often problematic. There is also a need to "stress test" balance sheets with alternative valuations when market prices for assets are not available or are subject to bubbles and bursts. Some more direct non-monetary indicators may be preferable when the monetary valuation is very uncertain or difficult to derive.

Recommendation 4: Give more prominence to the distribution of income, consumption and wealth.

Average income, consumption and wealth are meaningful statistics, but they do not tell the whole story about living standards. For example, a rise in average income could be unequally shared across groups, leaving some households relatively worse-off than others. Thus, average measures of income, consumption and wealth should be accompanied by indicators that reflect their distribution. Median consumption (income, wealth) provides a better measure of what is happening to the "typical" individual or household than average consumption (income or wealth). But for many purposes, it is also important to know what is happening at the bottom of the income/wealth distribution (captured in poverty statistics), or at the top. Ideally, such information should not come in isolation but be linked, i.e., one would like information about how well-off households are with regard to different dimensions of material living standards:

income, consumption and wealth. After all, a low-income household with above-average wealth is not necessarily worse-off than a medium-income household with no wealth. (The desirability of providing information on the "joint distribution" of the dimensions of people's well-being will be raised once again in the recommendations below on how to measure quality of life.)

Recommendation 5: Broaden income measures to non-market activities.

There have been major changes in how households and society function. For example, many of the services people received from other family members in the past are now purchased on the market. This shift translates into a rise in income as measured in the national accounts and may give a false impression of a change in living standards, while it merely reflects a shift from non-market to market provision of services. Many services that households produce for themselves are not recognized in official income and production measures, yet they constitute an important aspect of economic activity. While their exclusion from official measures reflects uncertainty about data more than conceptual difficulties, there has been progress in this arena; still, more and more systematic work in this area should be undertaken. This should start with information on how people spend their time that is comparable both over the years and across countries. Comprehensive and periodic accounts of household activity as satellites to the core national accounts should complement the picture. In developing countries, the production of goods (for instance food or shelter) by households plays an important role. Tracking the production of such home-produced goods is important to assess consumption levels of households in these countries.

Once one starts focusing on non-market activities, the question of leisure arises. Consuming the same bundle of goods and services but working for 1500 hours a year instead of 2000 hours a year implies an increase in one's standard of living. Although valuation of leisure is fraught with difficulties, comparisons of living standards over time or across countries needs to take into account the amount of leisure that people enjoy.

Well-Being Is Multidimensional

To define what well-being means a multidimensional definition has to be used. Based on academic research and a number of concrete initiatives developed around the world, the Commission has identified the following key dimension that should be taken into account. At least in principle, these dimensions should be considered simultaneously:

    i. Material living standards (income, consumption and wealth);
    ii. Health;
    iii. Education;
    iv. Personal activities including work;
    v. Political voice and governance;
    vi. Social connections and relationships;
    vii. Environment (present and future conditions);
    viii. Insecurity, of an economic as well as a physical nature.

All these dimensions shape people's well-being, and yet many of them are missed by conventional income measures.

Objective and Subjective Dimensions of Well-Being Are Both Important

Recommendation 6: Quality of life depends on people's objective conditions and capabilities. Steps should be taken to improve measures of people's health, education, personal activities and

environmental conditions. In particular, substantial effort
should be devoted to developing and implementing robust, reliable
measures of social connections, political voice and insecurity that can
be shown to predict life satisfaction.

The information relevant to valuing quality of life goes beyond people's self-reports and perceptions to include measures of their "functionings" and freedoms. In effect, what really matters are the capabilities of people, that is, the extent of their opportunity set and of their freedom to choose among this set, the life they value. The choice of relevant functionings and capabilities for any quality of life measure is a value judgment, rather than a technical exercise. But while the precise list of the features affecting quality of life inevitably rests on value judgments, there is a consensus that quality of life depends on people's health and education, their everyday activities (which include the right to a decent job and housing), their participation in the political process, the social and natural environment in which they live and the factors shaping their personal and economic security. Measuring all these features requires both objective and subjective data. The challenge in all these fields is to improve upon what has already been achieved, to identify gaps in available information, and to invest in statistical capacity in areas (such as time-use) where available indicators remain deficient.

Recommendation 7: Quality-of-life indicators in all the dimensions
covered should assess inequalities in a comprehensive way.

Inequalities in human conditions are integral to any assessment of quality of life across countries and the way that it is developing over time. Most dimensions of quality of life require appropriate separate measures of inequality, but, as noted earlier, taking into account linkages and correlations. Inequalities in quality of life should be assessed across people, socio-economic groups, gender and generations, with special attention to inequalities that have arisen more recently, such as those linked to immigration.

Recommendation 8: Surveys should be designed to assess the links between various quality-of-life domains for each person, and this information should be used when designing policies in various fields. It is critical to address questions about how developments in one domain of quality of life affect other domains, and how developments in all the various fields are related to income. This is important because the consequences for quality of life of having multiple disadvantages far exceed the sum of their individual effects. Developing measures of these cumulative effects requires information on the "joint distribution" of the most salient features of quality of life across everyone in a country through dedicated surveys. Steps in this direction could also be taken by including in all surveys some standard questions that allow classifying respondents based on a limited set of characteristics. When designing policies in specific fields, impacts on indicators pertaining to different quality-of-life dimensions should be considered jointly, to address the interactions between dimensions and the needs of people who are disadvantaged in several domains

Recommendation 9: Statistical offices should provide the information needed to aggregate across quality-of-life dimensions, allowing the construction of different indices. While assessing quality of life requires a plurality of indicators, there are strong demands to develop a single summary measure. Several summary measures of quality of life are possible, depending on the question addressed and the approach taken. Some of these measures are already being used, such as average levels of life-satisfaction for a country as a whole, or composite indices that aggregate averages across objective domains, such as the Human

Development Index. Others could be implemented if national statistical systems made the necessary investment to provide the data required for their computation. These include measures of the proportion of one's time in which the strongest reported feeling is a negative one, measures based on counting the occurrence and severity of various objective features of people's lives and (equivalent-income) measures based on people's states and preferences.

The Commission believes that in addition to objective indicators of well-being, subjective measures of the quality of life should be considered.

Recommendation 10: Measures of both objective and subjective well-being provide key information about people's quality of life. Statistical offices should incorporate questions to capture people's life-evaluations, hedonic experiences and priorities in their own survey.

Research has shown that it is possible to collect meaningful and reliable data on subjective as well as objective well-being. Subjective well-being encompasses different aspects (cognitive evaluations of one's life, happiness, satisfaction; positive emotions such as joy and pride and negative emotions such as pain and worry): each of them should be measured separately to derive a more comprehensive appreciation of people's lives. Quantitative measures of these subjective aspects hold the promise of delivering not just a good measure of quality of life *per se*, but also a better understanding of its determinants, reaching beyond people's income and material conditions. Despite the persistence of many unresolved issues, these subjective measures provide important information about quality of life. Because of this, the types of questions that have proved their value within small-scale and unofficial surveys should be included in larger-scale surveys undertaken by official statistical offices.

Use a Pragmatic Approach Towards Measuring Sustainability

Measuring and assessing sustainability has been a central concern of the Commission. Sustainability poses the challenge of determining if at least the current level of well-being can be maintained for future generations. By its very nature, sustainability involves the future and its assessment involves many assumptions and normative choices. This is further complicated by the fact that at least some aspects of environmental sustainability (notably climate change) is affected by interactions between the socio-economic and environmental models followed by different countries. The issue is indeed complex, more complex than the already complicated issue of measuring current well-being or performance.

Recommendation 11: Sustainability assessment requires a well-identified dashboard of indicators. The distinctive feature of the components of this dashboard should be that they are interpretable as variations of some underlying "stocks." A monetary index of sustainability has its place in such a dashboard but, under the current state of the art, it should remain essentially focused on economic aspects of sustainability.

The assessment of sustainability is complementary to the question of current well-being or economic performance, and must be examined separately. This may sound trivial and yet it deserves emphasis, because some existing approaches fail to adopt this principle, leading to potentially confusing messages. For instance, confusion may arise when one tries to combine current well-being and sustainability into a single indicator. To take an analogy, when driving a car, a meter that added up in one single number the current speed of the vehicle and the remaining level of gasoline would not be of any help to the driver. Both pieces of information are critical and need to be displayed in distinct, clearly visible areas of the dashboard.

At a minimum, in order to measure sustainability, what we need are indicators that inform us about the change in the quantities of the different factors that matter for future well-being. Put differently, sustainability requires the simultaneous preservation or increase in several "stocks": quantities and qualities of natural resources, and of human, social and physical capital.

There are two versions to the stock approach to sustainability. One version just looks at variations in each stock separately, assessing whether the stock is increasing or decreasing, with a view particularly to doing whatever is necessary to keep each above some critical threshold. The second version converts all these assets into a monetary equivalent, thereby implicitly assuming substitutability between different types of capital, so that a decrease in, say, natural capital might be offset by a sufficient increase in physical capital (appropriately weighted). Such an approach has significant potential, but also several limitations, the most important being the absence of many markets on which valuation of assets could be based. Even when there are market values, there is no guarantee that they adequately reflect how the different assets matter for future well-being. The monetary approach requires imputations and modeling which raise informational difficulties. All this suggests starting with a more modest approach, i.e., focusing the monetary aggregation on items for which reasonable valuation techniques exist, such as physical capital, human capital and certain natural resources. In so doing, it should be possible to assess the "economic" component of sustainability, that is, whether or not countries are overconsuming their economic wealth.

Physical Indicators for Environmental Pressures

Recommendation 12: The environmental aspects of sustainability deserve a separate follow-up based on a well-chosen set of physical indicators. In particular there is a need for a clear indicator of our proximity to dangerous levels of environmental damage (such as associated with climate change or the depletion of fishing stocks).

For the reasons mentioned above, placing a monetary value on the natural environment is often difficult and separate sets of physical indicators will be needed to monitor the state of the environment. This is particularly the case when it comes to irreversible and/or discontinuous alterations to the environment. For that reason members of the Commission believe in particular that there is a need for a clear indicator of increases in atmospheric concentrations of greenhouse gases associated with proximity to dangerous levels of climate change (or levels of emissions that might reasonably be expected to lead to such concentrations in the future). Climate change (due to increases in atmospheric concentrations of greenhouse gases) is also special in that it constitutes a truly global issue that cannot be measured with regard to national boundaries. Physical indicators of this kind can only be identified with the help of the scientific community. Fortunately, a good deal of work has already been undertaken in this field.

What Is Next?

The Commission regards its report as opening a discussion rather than closing it. The report hints at issues that ought to be addressed in the context of more comprehensive research efforts. Other bodies, at the national and international level, should discuss the recommendations in this report, identify their limits and see how best they can contribute to this broad agenda, each from its own perspective.

The Commission believes that a global debate around the issues and recommendations raised in this report provides an important venue for a discussion of societal values, for what we, as a society, care about, and whether we are really striving for what is important.

At the national level, round-tables should be established, with the involvement of stakeholders, to identify and prioritize those indicators that carry to potential for a shared view of how social progress is happening and how it can be sustained over time.

The Commission hopes that this report will provide the impetus not only for this broader discussion, but for ongoing research into the development of better metrics that will enable us to assess better economic performance and social progress.

1

CLASSICAL GDP ISSUES[1]

Introduction

Gross domestic product (GDP) is the most widely used measure of economic activity. There are international standards for its calculation, and much thought has gone into its statistical and conceptual bases. But GDP mainly measures *market* production, though it has often been treated as if it were a measure of economic well-being. Conflating the two can lead to misleading indications about how well-off people are and entail the wrong policy decisions.

One reason why money measures of economic performance and living standards have come to play such an important role in our societies is that the monetary valuation of goods and services makes it easy to add up quantities of a very different nature. When we know the prices of apple juice and DVD players, we can add up their values and make statements about production and consumption in a single figure. But market prices are more than an accounting device. Economic theory tells us that when markets are functioning properly, the ratio of one market price to another is reflective of the relative appreciation of the two products by those who purchase them. Moreover, GDP captures all final goods in the economy, whether they are consumed by households, firms or government. Valuing them with their prices would thus seem to be a good way of capturing, in a single number, how well-off society is at a particular moment. Furthermore, keeping prices unchanged while observing how quantities of goods and services that enter GDP move over time would seem like a reasonable way of making a statement about how society's living standards are evolving in real terms.

As it turns out, things are more complicated. First, prices may not exist for some goods and services (if for instance government provides free health insurance or if households are engaged in child care), raising the question of how these services should be valued. Second, even where there are market prices, they may deviate from society's underlying valuation. In particular, when the consumption or production of particular products affects society as a whole, the price that individuals pay for those products will differ from their value to society at large. Environmental damage caused by production or consumption activities that is not reflected in market prices is a well-known example.

There is yet another problem. While talking about the concepts of "prices" and "quantities" might be straightforward, defining and measuring how they change in practice is an altogether different matter. As it happens, many products change over time—they disappear entirely or new features are added to them. *Quality change* can be very rapid in areas like information and communication technologies. There are also products whose quality is complex, multidimensional and hard to measure, such as medical services, educational services, research activities and financial services. Difficulties also arise in collecting data in an era when an increasing fraction of sales take place over the internet and at sales as well as discount stores. As a consequence, capturing quality change correctly is a tremendous challenge for statisticians, yet this is vital to measuring real income and real consumption, some of the key determinants of people's well-being. Underestimating quality improvements is equivalent to overestimating the rate of inflation, and therefore to underestimating real income. For instance, in the mid-1990s, a report reviewing the measurement of inflation in the United States (Boskin Commission Report) estimated that insufficient accounting for quality improvements in goods and services had led to an annual overestimation of inflation by 0.6%. This led to a series of changes to the U.S. consumer price index.

The debate in Europe has tended to go the opposite way: official price statistics have been criticized for *underestimating* inflation. This has been partly because people's perception of inflation differs from the national averages presented in the consumer price index, and also because it is felt that statisticians overadjust for quality improvements in products, thereby painting too rosy a picture of citizens' real income.

For market prices to be reflective of consumers' appreciation of goods and services, it is also necessary that consumers are free to choose and that they dispose of the relevant information. It takes little imagination to argue that this is not always the case. Complex financial products are an example where consumer ignorance prevents market prices from playing their role as carriers of correct economic signals. The complex and ever-changing bundles of services offered by telecommunications companies are another case in point where it is difficult to ensure the transparency and comparability of price signals.

All the above considerations imply that price signals have to be interpreted with care in temporal and spatial comparisons. For a number of purposes, they do not provide a useful vehicle for the aggregation of quantities. This does not imply that the use of market prices in constructing measures of economic performance is generally flawed. But it does suggest prudence, in particular with regard to the often overemphasized measure, GDP.

This chapter suggests five ways of dealing with some of the deficiencies of GDP as an indicator of living standards. First, emphasize well-established indicators other than GDP in the national accounts. Second, improve the empirical measurement of key production activities, in particular the provision of health and education services. Third, bring out the household perspective, which is most pertinent for considerations of living standards. Fourth, add information about the distribution of income, consumption and wealth to data on the average evolution of these elements. Finally, widen the scope of what is being measured. In particular, a significant part of economic activity takes place outside markets and is often not reflected in established national accounts. However, when there are no markets, there are no market prices, and valuing such activities requires estimates ("imputations"). These are meaningful, but they come at a cost, and we shall discuss them before turning to the other proposals.

Imputations—Comprehensiveness Versus Comprehensibility

Imputations exist for two related reasons. The first is comprehensiveness. There are productive activities and associated income flows (typically non-monetary) that take place outside the market sphere, and some of them have been incorporated into GDP. The single most important imputation is a consumption value for the services that home-owners derive from living in their own dwellings. There is no market transaction and no payment takes place, but the national accounts treat this situation as if home-owners paid a rent to themselves. Most people would agree that if two persons receive the same money income but one of them lives in his/her own house while the other rents, they are not equally well-off—hence the imputation in order to better compare incomes over time or between countries. This brings us to the second reason for imputations, the *invariance principle*: the value of the main accounting aggregates should not depend on the institutional arrangements in a country. For example, if exactly the same medical services are provided in one case by the public sector and in another case by the private sector, overall measures of production should be unaffected by a switch between the two institutional settings. The main advantage of adhering to the invariance principle is better comparability over time and between countries. Therefore, for instance, measures of "adjusted disposable income" for households (see below) include an imputation for government services provided directly to citizens.

The imputations can be smaller or larger, depending on the country and on the national accounts aggregate considered. In France and Finland, for example, the main imputations account for about one-third of adjusted household disposable income and for just over 20% in the United States. Thus, in the absence of imputations the living standards of French and Finnish households would be understated relative to the United States.

But imputations come at a price. One is data quality: imputed values tend to be less reliable than observed values. Another is the effect of imputations on the comprehensibility of national accounts. Not all imputations are perceived as income-equivalent by people, and the result may be a discrepancy between changes in perceived income and changes in measured income. This problem is exacerbated when we widen the scope of economic activity to include other services that are not mediated by the market. Our estimates below for household work amount to around 30% of conventionally-measured GDP. Another 80% or so are added when leisure is valued as well. It is undesirable to have assumption-driven data so massively influencing overall aggregates.

There is no easy way out of the tension between comprehensiveness and comprehensibility except to keep both elements of information available for users and to maintain a distinction between core and satellite accounts. A full set of household accounts, for example, may not be well placed in the core of national accounts aggregates. But a satellite account that comes up with a valuation of comprehensive forms of household production would represent a significant improvement.

What Can Be Done Within the Existing Measurement Framework?

Emphasize National Accounts Aggregates Other Than GDP

A first step towards mitigating some of the criticism of GDP as a measure of living standards is to emphasize national accounts aggregates other than GDP, for example, by accounting for depreciation so as to deal with *net rather than gross measures* of economic activity.

Gross measures take no account of the depreciation of capital goods. If a large amount of output produced has to be set aside to renew machines and other capital goods, society's ability to consume is less than it would have been if only a small amount of set-aside were needed. The reason that economists have relied more heavily on GDP than on net domestic product (NDP) is, in part, that depreciation is hard to estimate. When the structure of production remains the same, GDP and NDP move closely together. But in recent years, the structure of production has changed. Information technology (IT) assets have gained importance as capital goods. Computers and software have a shorter life expectancy than do steel mills. On those grounds, the discrepancy between GDP and NDP may be increasing, and by implication, volume NDP may be increasing less rapidly than GDP. For example, real GDP in the United States rose by about 3% per year during the period 1985–2007. Depreciation rose by 4.4% over the same period. As a consequence, real net national product grew at a somewhat slower rate than GDP.

Of greater concern for some countries is that standard depreciation measures have not taken into account the degradation in quality of the natural environment. There have been various attempts to widen the scope of depreciation to reflect environmental degradation (or improvements, if such is the case), but without much success. The hurdle is the reliable measurement and monetary valuation of changes in environmental quality.

The case of natural resource depletion is slightly different—there is at least a market price, even if it does not reflect environmental damage attributable to the use of the natural resource. Depletion could be captured by excluding the value of the natural resources harvested from the production value of sectors like mining and timber. Their production would then consist only in a pure extraction or logging activity, with a corresponding decrease in GDP. A second possibility would be to take resource depletion into account in depreciation measures. In this case, GDP would be unchanged, but NDP would be lower.

In a world of globalization, there may be large differences between the *income* of a country's citizens and measures of domestic *production*, but the former is clearly more relevant for measuring the well-being of citizens. We shall argue later that the household sector is particularly relevant for our considerations, and for households the income perspective is much more appropriate than measures of production. Some of the income generated by residents is sent abroad, and some residents receive income from abroad. These flows are captured by *net national disposable income*, a standard variable in national accounts. Figure 1.1 shows how Ireland's income declines relative to its GDP—a reflection of an increasing share of profits that are repatriated by foreign investors. While the profits are included in GDP, they do not enhance the spending power of the country's citizens. For a poor developing country to be told that its GDP has gone up may be of little relevance. It wants to know whether its citizens are better-off, and national income measures are more relevant to this question than GDP.

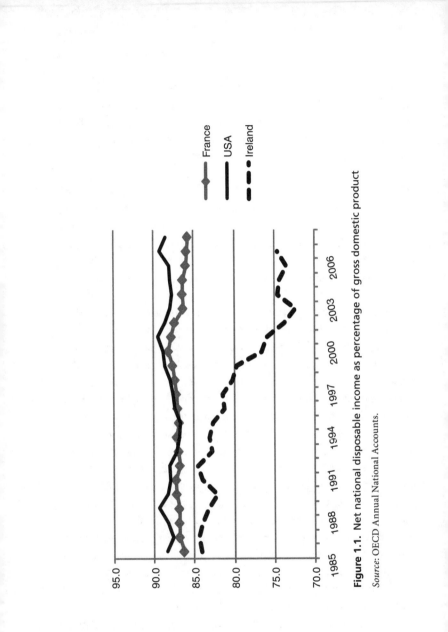

Figure 1.1. Net national disposable income as percentage of gross domestic product

Source: OECD Annual National Accounts.

Moreover, the prices of imports evolve very differently from the prices of exports, and these changes in relative prices have to be taken into account in assessing living standards. Figure 1.2 shows the divergence between real income and production in Norway, an oil-rich OECD country whose income has risen faster than GDP in times of rising oil prices. In many developing countries, whose export prices have tended to fall relative to import prices, the opposite will be true.

Improving the Measurement of Services in General

In today's economies, services account for up to two-thirds of total production and employment, yet measuring the prices and volumes of services is more difficult than for goods. Retail services are a case in point. In principle, numerous aspects should be taken into account in measuring the services provided: the volume of goods transacted but also the quality of service (accessibility of the shop, general service level of the staff, choice and presentation of products and so forth). It is difficult even to define these services, let alone to measure them. Statistical offices generally use data on the volume of sales as indicators for the volume of trade services. This method leaves aside most quality change in the trade services provided. What is true for retail holds for many other service industries, including those that are often publicly provided, such as health and education. A greater effort will be needed to come to grips with tracking the quantity and quality of services in modern economies.

Improving the Measurement of Government-Provided Services in Particular

Governments play an important part in today's economies. Broadly speaking, they provide two types of services—those of a "collective" nature, such as security, and those of an "individual"

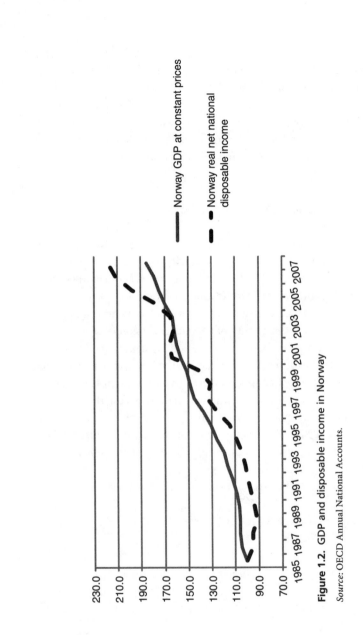

Figure 1.2. GDP and disposable income in Norway

Source: OECD Annual National Accounts.

nature, such as medical services and education. This does not imply that government is necessarily the only provider of these services, and indeed, the mix between private and public provision of individual services varies significantly across countries. And while one can argue about the contribution of collective services to citizens' living standards, individual services, particularly education, medical services and public sports facilities, are almost certainly valued positively by citizens. These services tend to be large in scale but badly measured. Traditionally, for government-provided non-market services, measures have been based on the inputs used to produce these services rather than on the actual outputs produced. An immediate consequence of this procedure is that productivity change for government-provided services is ignored, because outputs are taken to move at the same rhythm as inputs. It follows that if there is positive productivity growth in the public sector, our measures underestimate growth.

Work has started in many countries to develop output measures for these government-provided services that are independent of inputs, but the task is formidable. Take the following example: the United States spends more per capita on health care than many European countries, yet in terms of standard health indicators, outcomes are worse. Does this mean that Americans receive less health care? Or does it mean their health care is more expensive and/or delivered less efficiently? Or does it mean that health outcomes also depend on factors specific to American society other than health expenditure? We need to break down the change in health expenditure into a price and an output effect. But what exactly are the volumes of output that one is looking for? It is tempting to measure them by the population's state of health. The problem is that the link between health care expenditure and health status is tenuous at best: expenditures relate to the resources that go into the institutions providing health services, whereas the health status of the population is driven by many factors—and the situation is much the same for education. For example, people's lifestyles will affect health outcomes, and the time parents spend with their children will affect exam scores. Attributing changes in health or education status solely to hospitals or schools and the money spent on them neglects all these factors and can be misleading.

The quest is for more accurate measures of the volume growth of public services. A number of European countries as well as Australia and New Zealand have developed output-based measures for key government-provided services. One major challenge to these efforts is, once again, to capture quality change. Without a good measure of quality (or equivalently, a good estimate of increases in productivity), it is impossible to ascertain whether the conventional input measures underestimate or overestimate growth. If undifferentiated quantity measures are used, such as a simple number of students or of patients, changes in the composition and quality of the output may be missed. But one has to start somewhere and, because the numbers involved are important, the issue cannot be ignored, For example, with output-based measures, the UK economy grew at a rate of 2.75% per year between 1995 and 2003, whereas if the previous convention had continued to be used, the growth rate would have been 3% (Atkinson 2005). Similar effects could be observed in the case of France. A Danish study on the measurement of health output points the other way: output-based production of health services grew more rapidly than input-based production (Figure 1.3).

An important criterion for the reliability of output-based measures is that they are based on observations that are detailed enough to avoid mixing up true volume changes with compositional effects. We can ask how many students are educated, and simply count their numbers. If spending per student increases, one might conclude that the unit cost of educational services has increased. This may be misleading, however, if costs have gone up because students are taught in smaller classes or if there is a larger

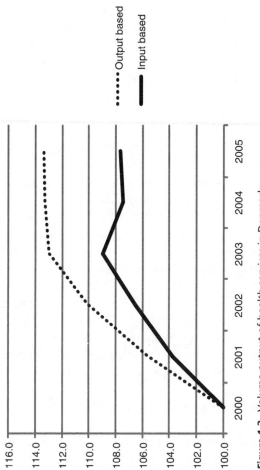

Figure 1.3. Volume output of health services in Denmark

Source: Deveci, Heurlén and Sorensen (2008) "Non-Market Health Care Service in Denmark—Empirical Studies of A, B and C Methods"; paper presented at the meeting of the International Association for Research on Income and Wealth, Slovenia.

share of students that take up engineering studies, which are more costly. The measurement mistake arises because the simple number of students is too undifferentiated an output measure to be meaningful, so a more detailed structure is needed. It would help, for instance, to treat one hour taught to a graduate engineering student as a different product from one hour taught to a first-year arts student, and thus to account for some quality and compositional change. A similar reasoning applies for health care: the treatments of different diseases have to be considered as different medical services. As it turns out, the health-care systems of some countries do provide the administrative data needed to obtain this detailed information. We conclude that despite this being a daunting task, the better measurement of government-provided individual services is central to the better assessment of living standards. Exploiting new administrative data sources is one way of making progress in this direction. Ideally, the information would also capture service quality, for instance, the way patients are accommodated in hospitals or the time devoted to them by the medical staff, though such data may be hard to collect. In this case, new primary data sources such as surveys may be necessary.

Improving the volume measures of outputs does not dispense with the need to improve—and publish—the volume measures of inputs. Only if both the outputs and inputs of service production are well captured will it be possible to estimate productivity change and undertake productivity comparisons across countries.

Revisit the Concept of "Defensive" Expenditures

Expenditures required to maintain consumption levels or the functioning of society could be viewed as a sort of intermediate input—there is no direct benefit, and in this sense they do not give rise to a final good or service. Nordhaus and Tobin, in their seminal 1973 paper, for example, identify as "defensive" those activities that "are evidently not directly sources of utility themselves but are regret-tably necessary inputs to activities that may yield utility." In partic-ular, they adjust income downwards for expenditures that arise as a consequence of urbanization and a complex modern life. Many such "defensive expenditures" are incurred by government, while others are incurred by the private sector. By way of example, ex-penditure on prisons could be considered a government-incurred defensive expenditure and the costs of commuting to work a privately-incurred defensive expenditure. A number of authors have suggested treating these expenditures as intermediate rather than final products. Consequently, they would not be part of GDP.

At the same time, difficulties abound when it comes to identify-ing which expenditures are "defensive" and which are not. For in-stance, if a new park is opened, does this constitute defensive expenditure against the disamenities of urban life or is it a non-defensive recreational service? What are the possible ways for-ward? Some options include:

First, focus on household consumption rather than total final con-sumption. For many purposes, the former is a more meaning-ful variable. And all of governments' collective consumption expenditures (which would include things like prisons, mili-tary expenditure and the clean-up of oil spills) are automati-cally excluded from household final consumption.

Second, widen the asset boundary. In many cases, defensive ex-penditures include elements of *investment* and *capital* goods. In those cases, they should be treated much like maintenance expenditures in the case of conventional production. For example, health expenditures could be seen as investment in human capital instead of as final consumption. If there is an asset that captures environmental quality, expenditures made to improve or maintain it could also be considered an invest-ment. Conversely, the consequences of economic activity that is detrimental to this asset could be captured in an extended measure of depreciation or depletion so that the *net* measure of income or production is reduced accordingly. And net measures, it was argued earlier, should be our benchmark for living standards rather than gross measures.

Third, widen the household production boundary. Some "defensive" expenditures cannot reasonably be treated as an investment. Take the case of commuting to work. Households produce transportation services—they use their time (labor input) and money (commuter ticket) for this purpose. With the exception of the consumer's purchase of a ticket for a commuter train, which counts as final consumption, none of the above flows enter measures of production and income. This could be remedied by allowing for the household production of transportation services, which would be considered as an unpaid delivery of intermediate inputs to firms, "subsidized" by private households. Although this treatment would not change overall GDP, it would show a larger contribution to production by households and a smaller contribution by firms.

The biggest obstacle to these approaches lies in their implementation. How exactly should the scope of defensive expenditures be determined? How should new assets and in-kind flows be valued? And, of course, widening the scope of asset and production measures brings with it more imputations.

Income, Wealth and Consumption Have to Be Considered Together

Income flows are an important gauge for the standard of living, but in the end it is consumption and consumption possibilities *over time* that matter. The time dimension brings in wealth. A low-income household with above-average wealth is better off than a low-income household without wealth. The existence of wealth is also one reason why income and consumption are not necessarily equal: for a given income, consumption can be raised by running down assets or by increasing debt, and consumption can be reduced by saving and adding to assets. For this reason, wealth is an important indicator of the sustainability of actual consumption.

The same holds for the economy as a whole. To construct the balance sheet of an economy, we need to have comprehensive accounts of its assets (physical capital—and probably human, natural and social capital) and its liabilities (what is owed to other countries). To know what is happening to the economy, we need to ascertain changes in wealth. In some instances, it may be easier to account for changes in wealth than to estimate the total value of wealth. Changes in wealth entail gross investments (in physical, natural, human and social capital) minus depreciation and depletion in those same assets.

Although information about some central aspects of household wealth is in principle available from national accounts balance sheets, it is often incomplete. Furthermore, certain assets are not recognized as such in the standard accounting framework, not least of all human capital. Studies that have computed monetary estimates of human capital stocks found that they account for an overwhelming part of all wealth (80% or more). A systematic measurement of human capital stock is of interest from a number of perspectives. It constitutes an integral part of an extended measure of household production (see below), and it is an input for the construction of sustainability indicators.

Note a fundamental problem with valuing stocks. When there are markets for assets, the prices at which assets are bought and sold serve to value the stock as a whole. But there may be no markets for certain assets or no trading on the markets, as has recently been the case for certain financial assets. This raises the question of how to value them. And even when market prices do exist, transactions correspond only to a small fraction of the existing stock, and they may be so volatile as to put a question mark on the interpretability of balance sheets. That said, basic information on assets and liabilities is key to assessing the economic health of the various sectors and the financial risks to which they are exposed.

Bringing Out the Household Perspective

Income can be computed for private households as well as for the economy as a whole. Some of citizens' income is taken away in the form of taxes, and so is not at their disposal. But the government takes this money away for a reason: to provide public goods and services, to invest, for example, in infrastructure and to transfer income to other (normally more needy) individuals. A commonly employed measure of household income adds and subtracts these transfer payments. The resulting measure is referred to as a measure of household disposable income. However, disposable income captures only monetary transfers between households and the government, thereby neglecting the in-kind services that government provides.

Adjusting Household Income Measures for Government Services in Kind

Earlier in this text we mentioned the invariance principle, according to which *a movement of an activity from the public to the private sector, or vice versa, should not change our measure of performance, except to the extent that there is an effect on quality or access.* This is where a purely market-based measure of income meets its limits and where a measure that corrects for differences in institutional arrangements may be warranted for comparisons over time or across countries. *Adjusted disposable income* is a national accounts measure that goes some way towards accommodating the invariance principle, at least where "social transfers in kind" by government are concerned.

The meaning of adjusted disposable income is best explained by way of an example (Table 1.1). Assume that a society's labor income equals 100 and that individuals who are active in the labor market buy private health insurance. They make an annual payment for the insurance equal to 10, which can be decomposed into 8 units of insurance premiums (the actuarial value of a payment of 8) and 2 units of consumption of insurance services. At the same time, persons who are sick receive 8 units as reimbursement of their health expenditures. In this case—let us call it Case A—no taxes are paid and insurance claims and premiums offset each other, so that household disposable income equals 100. Now, assume that the government decides to provide the same amount of health insurance coverage to everyone, funded through a tax of 10 units. Nothing has changed, other than that the government is now collecting the insurance payment and distributing the benefits

Table 1.1. Private and Public Insurance Schemes

	Private insurance scheme (Case A)	Public insurance scheme (Case B)
Labor income	100	100
Tax	0	–10
Insurance premiums (excluding insurance services)	–8	0
Insurance claims	+8	**0**
Household disposable income	100	90
Social transfers in kind:		+10
—reimbursements	0	+8
—running costs of the insurance		+2
Adjusted household disposable income	**100**	**100**

(Case B). But according to standard national accounts statistics, household disposable income has fallen, to 90 currency units. Thus, disposable income here yields a distorted comparison. If one adds in the social transfers in kind that households receive from the government under Case B (8 units corresponding to the reimbursement of health expenditures and 2 units corresponding to the running costs of the insurance), the adjusted measure of household disposable income indicates equality between the two cases.

The above example leaves aside, however, any consideration about which insurance regime operates more cost effectively and about the profits that might be made by private insurance companies—it was simply assumed that the private and public insurance services are equivalent to 2 currency units. In practice, this is almost certainly not the case, although it is difficult to make a general observation about the relative efficiency of such schemes. If the insurance services industry is not perfectly competitive (a reasonable assumption in most countries), the transfer of responsibility from the private to the public sector will be reflected in decreased profits and decreased insurance prices. Even if profits are distributed to households in the form of dividends, the change in the form of provision (from private to public) can increase the accessibility of the insurance service. Having an opportunity to insure against certain types of risks has a positive impact on the well-being of people who are risk adverse.

While the failure to estimate the value of the insurance services provided causes one set of biases, there are other biases that arise from the fact that the value of some social transfers in kind (those corresponding to the running costs of the insurance in the example above) is measured by the cost of producing these services. In some countries, in particular in the developing world, the cost of these services may greatly exceed their value to households, who may receive little or nothing. In this situation, the result of using adjusted household income would be a large-scale overestimation of the level of household income and consumption. Some of this can be tackled by using output-based volume measures for the health and education services produced by government. It is also likely that different parts of the population benefit unequally from social transfers in kind provided by government. There is thus an important distributional aspect.

Major items included in social transfers in kind are health and education services, subsidized housing, sport and recreation facilities and the like that are provided to citizens at a low price or for free. In France, general government provides nearly all of these services, which in 2007 cost about € 290 billion. Education and health services each account for about one-third of total transfers in kind, and housing and recreational and cultural activities (museums, public parks, etc.) account for about 10% (Figure 1.4).

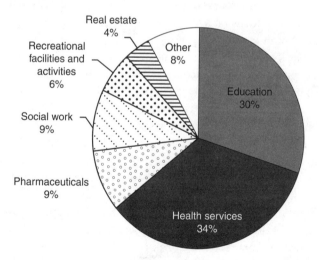

Figure 1.4. Social transfers in kind from general government, France 2007

Source: INSEE.

Medians and Means—Distribution of Income, Consumption and Wealth

Average measures of per-capita income and wealth give no indication of how the available resources are distributed across persons or households. Similarly, average consumption gives no indication of how people effectively benefit from these resources. For example, *average* income per capita can remain unchanged while the distribution of income becomes less equal. It is therefore necessary to look at disposable income, consumption and wealth information for different groups. A conceptually simple way of capturing distribution aspects is to measure *median* income (the income such that half of all individuals are above that income, and half below), median consumption and median wealth. The median individual is, in some sense, the "typical" individual. If inequality increases, the differences between medians and averages may well increase, so a focus on averages does not give an accurate picture of the economic well-being of the "typical" member of society. For example, if all the increases in societal income accrue, say, to those in the top 10%, median income may remain unchanged, while average income increases. Over the past two decades, the dominant pattern in OECD countries is one of a fairly widespread increase in income inequality, with strong rises in Finland, Norway, Sweden (from a low base) and Germany, Italy, New Zealand and the United States (from a high base). In these cases, medians and means would give different pictures of what is happening to societal well-being. Alternatively, changes in the disposable income of different income groups can be tracked. Such an approach would, for instance, look at the numbers of people below a critical income level, or the average income of those in the bottom or top decile. Similar calculations would be useful for consumption and wealth. Empirical research has repeatedly shown that the distribution of consumption can be quite different from the distribution of income. Indeed, the most pertinent measures of the distribution of material living standards are probably based on *jointly* considering the income, consumption and wealth position of households or individuals.

In practice, moving from averages to medians is more difficult than meets the eye. Measures of averages are obtained by dividing aggregates by a population figure. To consider distributional elements, micro-economic information is needed that provides information for individual households or groups of households. Micro-economic measures refer to people living in private households and are typically derived from household income surveys, whereas macro-economic measures from the national accounts are based on a range of different sources, and include people living in collective households (such as prisons and institutions for long-term care).

An important choice also concerns the unit of measurement. Macro-estimates give totals for a whole country or sector, while micro-data retain the household (or the family) as the unit within which resources are pooled and shared, and adjust income for differences in "needs." There are, for instance, fixed costs to running a household, allowing larger families with the same per-capita income to have a higher standard of living. Another step towards bringing demography and some distributional aspects into income measures is to calculate disposable income per consumption unit rather than per person. Consumption units are households whose size has been adjusted to take account of economies of scale in housing and other costs. This adjustment is of increasing importance as household size shrinks.

Against this background, we can consider the evolution of average and median household income in several countries (Figure 1.5). Average income per capita and average income per consumption

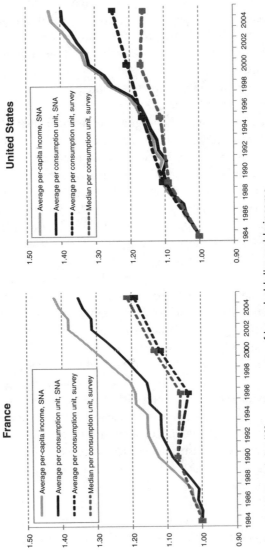

Figure 1.5. Trends in different measures of household disposable income

Source: Computations based on OECD SNA and income distribution data.

unit diverge, reflecting a trend towards a smaller household size. Survey income measures permit comparing average and median income. In the case of France, these two items move in parallel. At least from this perspective, there is no indication of a widening income distribution. The picture is different for the United States, where average income per capita and per consumption unit grow at the same rate but where there is a widening gap between median and average income, pointing to a more unequal income distribution.

There are many measurement issues that can influence the above statements. One source of discrepancy between micro- and macro-estimates is property income, whether imputed or not. If this aggregate is not well measured in micro-estimates, this could explain why average and median incomes in these estimates move in parallel in France, where wage inequalities are less important than property income inequalities. In addition, there is a possibility that top incomes are underrepresented in household income surveys. Finally, the international comparability between household surveys is far from perfect.

From the perspective of living standards, what matters is that the distribution of income, consumption and wealth determines who enjoys access to the goods and services produced within a society. Complementing measures of average income by measures with a distributional element is thus a crucial task for official statistics. Ideally, such distributional measures should be compatible in scope with average measures from the national accounts.

Similarly, the distribution of the volume of consumption is also important. The same dollar may buy different bundles of products, depending on the income group of the purchaser. Going from nominal to real income and from the value to the volume of consumption means applying a price index, raising the question of *whose price index* are we measuring. Conceptual discussions about price indices are often conducted as if there exists a single representative consumer. Statistical agencies calculate the increase in prices by looking at what it costs to purchase an average bundle of goods. The problem is that different people buy different bundles of goods, e.g., poor people spend more on food, and rich people on entertainment. People also buy goods and services in different types of stores, which sell "similar" products at very different prices. When all prices move together, having different indices for different people may not make much difference. But recently, with soaring oil and food prices, these differences have become marked. Those at the bottom may have seen real incomes be more affected than those at the top.

A price index for (actual) private consumption for major groups in society (age, income, rural/urban) is necessary if we are to appraise their economic situation. One of the recommendations of the *Commission sur la mesure du pouvoir d'achat des ménages* (2008) (Commission on the measurement of household purchasing power) in France was to develop consumer price indices for owners of dwellings, for households who rent dwellings and for households who are about to purchase dwellings. A full development of price indices differentiated by socio-economic group requires, however, that different prices be collected for different segments of the population, so that socio-economic aspects are taken into account in the data collection design. This is likely to prove difficult and costly, and should constitute a medium-term research objective—a recommendation that echoes a similar conclusion by the 2002 *Panel on Conceptual, Measurement, and Other Statistical Issues in Developing Cost-of-Living Indices* in the United States. Such work would not only enhance the quality of deflation procedures, it would also make it easier for citizens to compare their personal situation with some of the income and price data released by statistical offices.

Broader Measures of Household Economic Activity

There have been major changes in how households and society function. For example, many of the services people received from other family members in the past are now purchased on the market. This shift translates into a rise in income as measured in the national accounts and gives a false impression of a change in living standards, while it merely reflects a shift from non-market to market provision of services. Just as we argued that a shift from private to public provision of a particular good or service, or vice-versa, should not affect measured output, so too, a shift of production from household to market production, or vice-versa, should not affect measured output. We noted earlier that, in practice, current conventions do, however, lead to changes in measured income in both instances.

Imagine a two-parent household with two children and an income of 50,000 currency units a year, in which only one parent works full-time for pay and the other specializes in home production. The parent who stays at home does all the shopping, cooks all the meals, does all the cleaning, and performs all the child care. As a result, this household does not need to devote any of its market income to purchasing these services. Now imagine a two-parent household with two children in which *both* parents work full-time for the same global pay (50,000 a year), and neither parent has any time left over for household production or child care. They must pay for all the shopping, cooking, cleaning and child care out of pocket. Their available income is therefore reduced. Conventional measures treat these two households as if they have identical living standards, but obviously they don't. Focusing on market production provides a biased picture of living standards— some of the measured increase in market production may simply reflect a *shift* of the locus of production from households to the market.

To get a sense of how important home production is economically, one has to start by examining how people use their time. Figure 1.6. provides a first comparison of time spent per household and per day on various activities. Household production comprises time spent on housework, purchasing goods and services, caring for and helping household and non-household members, volunteer activities, telephone calls, mail and email and travel time related to all these activities. "Personal care" consists mainly of sleeping, eating and drinking, whereas leisure was defined to include sports, religious and spiritual activities and other leisure activities.

Based on these definitions, more time is spent on household production in European countries than in the United States, and more time is spent on leisure in Finland, France, Italy, Germany and the United Kingdom than in the United States (Figure 1.6). Note that some of the classifications are ambiguous, so the results should be read with care. For example, eating and drinking are included in the definition of personal care, whereas, arguably, some eating and drinking is time spent on leisure. The time-use picture would also change if eating time were allocated differently. We conclude that the allocation of specific activities to time-use categories as well as their international comparison leaves room for improvement and harmonization.

If we gloss over these issues, it is possible to come up with an illustrative calculation of the value of household production for France, Finland and the United States. The approach chosen here is simple: the value of the production of household services is measured by its cost. The value of labor is estimated by applying the wage rate of a generalist household worker to the number of hours that people spend on housework. Methodology matters in this context and results can differ markedly, depending in particular on the hypotheses chosen for the valuation of labor and

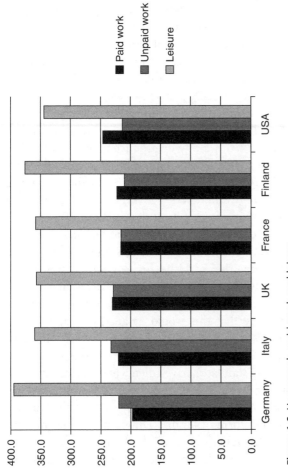

Figure 1.6. Housework, paid work and leisure

Minutes per day and person, latest year available*

Paid work
Unpaid work
Leisure

* Using normalized series for personal care; United States: 2005, Finland 1998, France 1999, Germany 2002, Italy 2003, United Kingdom 2001.

Source: OECD (2009), *Growing Unequal? Income Distribution and Poverty in OECD Countries;* Paris.

capital. We also lack estimates for productivity changes in household production.

However, our estimates do provide orders of magnitude. It is apparent, and no surprise in light of previous studies, that imputations for own-account production of household services are sizeable in all countries. Household production amounts to about 35% of conventionally-measured GDP in France (average 1995–2006), about 40% in Finland and 30% in the United States over the same period.

Once one starts thinking about non-market income, one also has to think about leisure. With time spent on generating income (market or non-market), we buy or produce goods and services to meet our needs or for simple enjoyment. Time available for leisure obviously affects well-being. Changes in the amount of leisure over time and differences between countries represent one of the more important aspects of the situation of well-being in these respects. Focusing only on goods and services can therefore bias comparative measures of living standards. This is of particular concern as the world begins to come to terms with environmental constraints. It may not be possible to increase the production, especially of goods, beyond limit, because of the environmental damage that this would entail. Taxes and regulations may be imposed that will discourage production. However, it would be a mistake if, as a result of these measures, we were to conclude that living standards have fallen when leisure time (and environmental quality) has increased. As society progresses, it is not unreasonable to expect people to enjoy some of the fruits of that progress in the form of leisure. Different societies may respond differently to higher living standards, and we do not want to bias our judgments (e.g., of success) *against* societies that choose to enjoy more leisure.

Measurement of the value of leisure starts, once again, from time-use data. We multiply the average leisure time per day by the working-age population and then by the average wage rate in the economy. Again, this procedure raises many measurement issues, but the purpose here is to show that estimates are feasible and can produce meaningful cross-country comparisons. For the three countries at hand, the value of leisure roughly doubles net household disposable income in nominal terms. More interesting than nominal income levels is the question of how considering leisure affects the measured growth rates of *real* income and their comparisons across countries. This is captured in Table 1.2. It shows the evolution of household income, now adjusted for household work (upper panel) and for household work and leisure (lower panel). For all countries, the new real income measures grow more slowly than the traditional measures of income. When expressed as income per consumption unit (i.e., per household, adjusted for household size), the income growth rates of the three countries turn out to be very similar.

Table 1.2. Household Income in Real Terms
Percentage change at annual rate, 1995–2006

	France	United States	Finland
Adjusted disposable income plus housework			
Total	1.9%	2.9%	2.0%
Per consumption unit	1.1%	1.7%	1.6%
Adjusted disposable income plus housework and leisure			
Total	1.4%	2.3%	1.4%
Per consumption unit	0.7%	1.0%	0.9%

The imprecision associated with the above estimates should be reiterated here. These are orders of magnitude at best and should not be overinterpreted. However, it is clear that the recognition of broader measures of economic activity and of leisure does make a difference to comparisons over time and between countries. More work needs to be done to test methodologies, to single out the most critical parameters and to test the robustness of such measures. Only if there is sufficient confidence in extended measures of income will there be a broader take-up by statistical offices.

More instructive than estimating the rate of change in real income is assessing how household production and leisure bear on the comparison of income *levels* across countries. Income levels should be compared in real terms, so we construct currency converters, so-called *Purchasing Power Parities (PPP)* that permit comparisons of "full" income (including housework and leisure) across countries. Figure 1.7 compares three income aggregates for France and the United States. The first comparison uses the established disposable income measure. Here, France's per-capita income is about 66% of the comparable United States figure. Adding in government-provided services such as health and education narrows the gap to 79%. If, in addition, housework and leisure are accounted for, one ends up with a relative income level of 87%.

Distribution of Full Income

It was argued earlier that measures of average income should be accompanied by measures that also provide distributional information. The rationale for examining income distribution holds for market income, but also for broader measures, such as full income. The recognition of the own-account production of

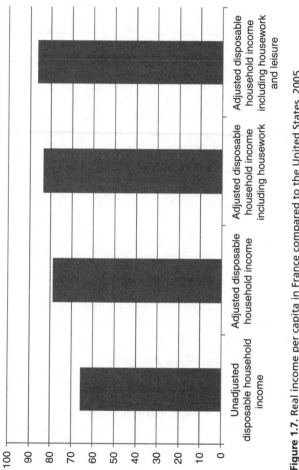

Figure 1.7. Real income per capita in France compared to the United States, 2005
United States=100

household services and leisure affects aggregate measures of income and production, but may also change the established picture of income distribution.

Developing distributional measures of full income is, however, a formidable task. The most difficult challenge is to allocate to various groups those income flows that have been imputed at the macro level when comprehensive measures of income were derived, for example, imputed rents from own-occupied housing. Other imputations for own-account services produced by households also fall under this category, as do the distributional effects of government services that are provided in kind.

Again, measurement difficulties should not prevent us from developing a more comprehensive picture of the distribution of income and wealth. The distribution of full income should be firmly anchored in the research agenda.

Main Messages and Recommendations

Recommendation 1: Look at income and consumption rather than production.

GDP is the most widely-used measure of economic activity. There are international standards for its calculation, and much thought has gone into its statistical and conceptual bases. But GDP mainly measures market production, though it has often been treated as if it were a measure of economic well-being. Conflating the two can lead to misleading indications about how well-off people are and entail the wrong policy decisions. Material living standards are more closely associated with measures of real income and consumption—production can expand while income decreases or vice versa when account is taken of depreciation, income flows into and out of a country, and differences between the prices of output and the prices of consumer products.

*Recommendation 2: Consider income and consumption
jointly with wealth.*

Income and consumption are crucial for assessing living standards, but in the end they can only be gauged in conjunction with information on wealth. A vital indicator of the financial status of a firm is its balance sheet, and the same holds for the economy as a whole. To construct the balance sheet of an economy, we need comprehensive accounts of its assets (physical capital—and probably even human, natural and social capital) and its liabilities (what is owed to other countries). Balance sheets for countries are not novel in concept, but their availability is still limited and their construction should be promoted. There is also a need to "stress test" balance sheets with alternative valuations when market prices for assets are not available or are subject to bubbles and bursts. Measures of wealth are also central to measuring sustainability. What is carried over into the future necessarily has to be expressed as stocks—of physical, natural, human or social capital. Here too the right valuation of these stocks plays a crucial role.

Recommendation 3: Emphasize the household perspective.

While it is informative to track the performance of economies as a whole, trends in citizens' material living standards are better followed through measures of household income and consumption. Indeed, the available national accounts data shows that in a number of OECD countries real household income has grown quite differently from real GDP, and typically at a lower rate. The household perspective entails taking account of payments between sectors, such as taxes going to government, social benefits coming from government and interest payments on household loans going to financial corporations. Properly defined, household income and consumption should also reflect the value of in-kind services provided by government, such as subsidized health care and educational services.

Recommendation 4: Give more prominence to the distribution of income, consumption and wealth.

Average income, consumption and wealth are meaningful statistics, but they do not tell the whole story about living standards. For example, a rise in average income could be unequally shared across groups, leaving some households relatively worse-off than others. Thus, average measures of income, consumption and wealth should be accompanied by indicators that reflect their distribution. Ideally, such information should not come in isolation but be linked, i.e., one would like information about how well-off households are with regard to all three dimensions of material living standards: income, consumption and wealth. After all, a low-income household with above-average wealth is not necessarily worse-off than a medium-income household with no wealth. The desirability of disposing of information on the "joint distribution" of dimensions will be encountered once again in Recommendation 3 of the chapter on the quality of life.

Recommendation 5: Broaden income measures to non-market activities.

There have been major changes in how households and society function. For example, many of the services people received from other family members in the past are now purchased on the market. This shift translates into a rise in income as measured in the national accounts and may give a false impression of a change in living standards, while it merely reflects a shift from non-market to market provision of services. Many services that households produce for themselves are not recognized in official income and production measures, yet they constitute an important aspect of economic activity. While their exclusion from official measures reflects uncertainty about data more than it does conceptual dissent, more and more systematic work in this area should be undertaken. This should start with information on how people spend their time that is comparable both over the years and across countries. Comprehensive and periodic accounts of household activity as satellites to the core national accounts should complement the picture.

2

QUALITY OF LIFE[2]

Introduction

Quality of life is a broader concept than economic production and living standards. It includes the full range of factors that influences what we value in living, reaching beyond its material side. While some extensions of economic accounting (discussed in chapter 1) allow including some of the elements that shape quality of life in conventional measures of economic well-being, every approach based on resources (or on people's command over commodities) remains limited in important ways. First, resources are means that are transformed into well-being in ways that differ across people: individuals with greater capacities for enjoyment or greater abilities for achievement in valuable domains of life may be better off even if they command fewer economic resources. Second, many resources are not marketed, and even when they are, prices will differ across individuals, making it problematic to compare real income across people. Finally, many of the determinants of human well-being are aspects of people's life-circumstances: they cannot be described as resources with imputable prices, even if people do make trade-offs among them. These arguments by themselves are sufficient to suggest that resources are an insufficient metric for quality of life. Which other metric should be used instead for assessing quality of life depends on the philosophical perspective taken.

While a long tradition of philosophical thought has addressed the issues of what gives life its quality, recent advances in research have led to measures that are both new and credible. This research suggests that the need to move beyond measures of economic resources is not limited to developing countries (the traditional focus of much work on "human development" in the past) but is even more salient for rich industrialized countries. These measures, while not *replacing* conventional economic indicators, provide an opportunity to *enrich* policy discussions and to inform people's view of the conditions of the communities where they live. More importantly, the new measures now have the potential to move from research to standard statistical practice. While some of them reflect structural conditions that are relatively invariant over time but that differ systematically across countries, others are more responsive to policies and more suitable for monitoring changes over shorter periods of time. Both types of indicator play an important role in evaluating quality of life.

Conceptual Approaches to Measuring Quality of Life

Three conceptual approaches have retained the attention of the Commission as useful in thinking about how to measure quality of life.

- The first approach, developed in close connection with psychological research, is based on the notion of *subjective well-being*. A long philosophical tradition views individuals as the best judges of their own conditions. This approach is closely linked to the utilitarian tradition but has a broader appeal due to the strong presumption in many streams of ancient and modern culture that enabling people to be "happy" and "satisfied" with their life is a universal goal of human existence.
- The second approach is rooted in the notion of *capabilities*. This approach conceives a person's life as a combination of

various "doings and beings" (functionings) and of his or her freedom to choose among these functionings (capabilities). Some of these capabilities may be quite elementary, such as being adequately nourished and escaping premature mortality, while others may be more complex, such as having the literacy required to participate actively in political life. The foundations of the capability approach, which has strong roots in philosophical notions of social justice, reflect a focus on human ends and on respecting the individual's ability to pursue and realize the goals that he or she values; a rejection of the economic model of individuals acting to maximize their self-interest heedless of relationships and emotions; an emphasis on the complementarities between various capabilities; and a recognition of human diversity, which draws attention to the role played by ethical principles in the design of the "good" society.

- The third approach, developed within the economics tradition, is based on the notion of *fair allocations*. The basic idea, which is common to welfare economics, is that of weighting the various non-monetary dimensions of quality of life (beyond the goods and services that are traded in markets) in a way that respects people's preferences. This approach requires choosing a particular reference point for each of the various non-monetary dimensions, and obtaining information on people's current situations and on their preferences with respect to these points. This approach avoids the pitfall of basing evaluations on an "average" willingness-to-pay that may disproportionately reflect the preferences of those who are better-off in society and focuses instead on equality among all of its members.

These approaches have obvious differences, but also certain similarities. For example, subjective well-being is sometimes claimed to encompass all capabilities, insofar as these refer to attributes and freedoms that people *value* (implying that enhancing their capabilities will improve people's subjective states). However, proponents of the capability approach also emphasize that subjective states are not the only things that matter, and that expanding people's opportunities is important in itself, even if this does not show up in greater subjective well-being. Similarly, both the capability and the fair allocation approaches rely on information on the objective attributes of each person, while differing in the ways in which these are weighted and aggregated. While the choice between these approaches is ultimately a normative decision, they all point to the importance of a number of features that go beyond command over resources. Measuring these features requires the use of types of data (i.e., responses to questionnaires and non-market observations of personal states) that are not captured by market transactions.

Subjective Measures of Quality of Life

For a long time, economists have assumed that it was sufficient to look at people's choices to derive information about their well-being, and that these choices would conform to a standard set of assumptions. In recent years, however, much research has focused on what people value and how they act in real life, and this has highlighted large discrepancies between standard assumptions of economic theory and real-world phenomena. A significant part of this research has been undertaken by psychologists and economists based on subjective data on people's reported or experienced well-being.

Subjective measures have always been part of the traditional tool-kit of economists and statisticians, as many features of our economies and societies are measured through people's responses to a standard set of questions (for example, "unemployment" is typically measured based on people's answers as to whether they worked at all in a specific reference week, whether they actively looked for a job and whether they would be available to start working in the near future). The specific feature of the subjective measures of quality of life discussed here is that what people report about their own conditions has no obvious objective counterpart: we can compare "perceived" and "actual" inflation, for example, but only respondents can provide information on their own subjective states and values. Despite this feature, a rich literature on these subjective measures concludes that they help to predict people's behavior (e.g., workers who report more dissatisfaction in their work are more likely to quit their job), and that they are valid with respect to a range of other information (e.g., people who report themselves as "happy" tend to smile more and to be rated as happy by people around them; these self-reports are also correlated with electrical readings of the brain).

Subjective approaches distinguish between the *dimensions* of quality of life and the objective *factors* shaping these dimensions. In turn, the subjective dimensions of quality of life encompass several aspects. The first is represented by people's evaluations of their life as a whole or of its various domains, such as family, work and financial conditions. These evaluations imply a cognitive exercise by each person and an effort to take stock of and summarize the full range of elements that people value (e.g., their sense of purpose, the fulfilment of their goals and how they are perceived by others). The second aspect is represented by people's actual feelings, such as pain, worry and anger, or pleasure, pride and respect. To the extent that these feelings are reported in real time, they are less affected by biases due to memory and to social pressure related to what is deemed to be "good" in society. Within this broad category of people's feelings, the research on subjective well-being distinguishes between positive and negative affects, as both characterize the experience of each person.

All these aspects of subjective well-being (cognitive evaluations, positive affects and negative affects) should be measured separately to get a satisfactory appreciation of people's lives. Which of these aspects matters more, and for what purpose, is still an open question. Much evidence suggests that people act to achieve satisfaction in their choices, and that choices are based on memories and evaluations. But memories and evaluations can also lead to bad choices, and some choices are made unconsciously rather than by weighing the pros and cons of various alternatives.

Subjective reports of people's life-evaluations and affects provide measures of quality of life that can be monitored over time; some of these measures can also be compared across countries in reliable ways. Probably more importantly, however, is that these measures provide information about the determinants of quality of life at the level of *each person*. These determinants include both features of the environment where people live and their individual conditions, and they vary depending on the aspect considered. For example, activities (such as commuting, working or socializing) may be more important for affects, while conditions (such as being married, or having a rewarding job) may be more important for life-evaluations. In both cases, however, these measures provide information beyond that conveyed by income. For example, in most developed countries younger and older people report higher evaluations of their life than prime-age people, a pattern that contrasts sharply with levels of income for the same groups.

One area where various subjective measures of people's well-being agree is in pointing to the high costs of unemployment for people's quality of life. People who become unemployed report lower life-evaluations, even after controlling for their lower income, and with little adaptation over time; unemployed people also report a higher prevalence of various negative affects (sadness, stress and pain) and lower levels of positive ones (joy). These subjective measures suggest that the costs of unemployment exceed the income-loss suffered by those who lose their jobs, reflecting the existence of non-pecuniary effects among the unemployed and of fears and anxieties generated by unemployment in the rest of society.

While the initiatives of individual researchers and commercial data providers have led to important advances in the measurement of subjective well-being, the data remain limited in terms of the statistical inferences that they allow. National statistical systems need to build on these efforts and incorporate questions about various aspects of subjective well-being in their standard surveys. They should also develop longitudinal studies that could support more valid inferences about the relative importance of the various factors at work.

Objective Features Shaping Quality of Life

Both the capability and the fair allocation approaches give prominence to people's objective conditions and the opportunities available to them, while differing in how these features are valued and ranked. While these objective features may also have an instrumental value for subjective well-being, both of these conceptual approaches regard an expansion of people's opportunities in these domains as intrinsically important for people's lives.

The range of objective features to be considered in any assessment of quality of life will depend on the purpose of the exercise: is the goal to assess changes in conditions within national jurisdictions, or to compare these conditions across countries at different levels of development? Some features may matter as descriptors of people's states (e.g., health), while others may reflect the freedoms that people have to pursue the goals that they value (e.g., political voice). While the question of which elements should belong to a list of objective features inevitably depends on value judgments, in practice most of these themes are shared across countries and constituencies, and there is a large degree of consistency among the various exercises that focus on measuring "well-being" and related concepts.[3] In general, measures for all these objective features highlight that how societies are organized makes a difference for people's lives, and that their influences are not all captured by conventional measures of economic resources.

Health

Health is a basic feature shaping both the length and the quality of people's lives. Its assessment requires good measures of both mortality and morbidity. Data gaps remain significant in both fields. Mortality statistics by age and gender document the risk of death confronting people and are used to calculate the expected length of a person's life. These indicators are today available in all developed countries but remain limited in large parts of the developing world, in particular for adults, which limits the possibility of monitoring progress in achieving the UN Millennium Development Goals. Further, age-specific mortality statistics are vectors: to obtain a scalar measure of people's lifespan, they need to be aggregated in suitable ways and standardized for differences in age-structure across countries and over time. While different aggregation formulas and standardization methods exist, they lead to different results and rankings when comparing countries with survival curves (by age) that cross each other. This suggests that a variety of mortality measures should be compiled and regularly monitored. Nonetheless, it is significant that non-monetary measures of people's health can diverge significantly from conventional economic measures. For example, although France has a lower GDP per capita than the United States, its life-expectancy at birth is higher, and this advantage has been widening (from less than 6 months in 1960 to almost 2 years in 2006) even while its GDP per capita relative to the U.S. was falling (Figure 2.1).

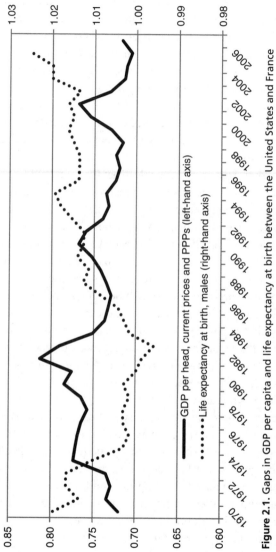

Figure 2.1. Gaps in GDP per capita and life expectancy at birth between the United States and France

Note: Ratios of French values to U.S. values (values greater than 1 indicate better conditions in France than in the U.S.). For example, in 2006 French GDP per capita was 0.82 of the U.S. level, while the life expectancy of French men was 1.025 times that of men in the United States.

Source: OECD data.

The state of progress is far more limited for statistics on morbidity, a situation that has led to long-standing disagreements about whether declines in mortality have been matched by similar declines in morbidity. Existing measures of morbidity rest on a variety of sources: records of people's height and weight; diagnoses by health professionals; registers for specific diseases; and self-reports drawn for censuses and surveys. Some of these measures relate to the prevalence of diseases or injuries, while others refer to their consequences in terms of the functioning of the person affected (which also depends on the quality of treatment). Variations in the measures and underlying data are inevitable given the many manifestations of poor health, but this also poses a real obstacle to comparing countries and monitoring changes in people's morbidity over time. Measures are even sparser when moving from physical to mental disorders, despite evidence that these affect (at least in mild forms) a large share of people, that most of these disorders go untreated, and that their incidence has been increasing in some countries.

The variety of dimensions of people's health has led to several attempts to define a summary measure that combines both mortality and morbidity. However, although several combined indices of people's health exist, none currently commands universal agreement. Further, they all inevitably rest on ethical judgments that are controversial, and on weights for various medical conditions whose legitimacy is not always clear.

The challenges posed by this variety of health measures are not confined to cross-country comparisons but extend to within-country comparisons. Recent research on inequalities in health status has highlighted several patterns. First, people from lower occupational classes who have less education and income tend to die at younger ages and to suffer, within their shorter lifetimes, a higher prevalence of various health problems. Second, these differences in health conditions do not merely reflect worse outcomes for people at the very bottom of the socio-economic scale but extend to people throughout the socio-economic hierarchy, i.e., they display a "social gradient": for example, life expectancy in the United Kingdom increases when moving from unskilled manual workers to skilled ones, from manual to non-manual workers, from lower-ranked office workers to higher-ranked staff. While these patterns in health inequalities have an obvious relevance for assessing quality of life, existing measures do not allow cross-country comparisons of their magnitude, due to differences in the measures of health outcomes used, in the individual characteristics considered (education, income, ethnicity), and in the reference population and geographic coverage of the various national studies.[4]

Education

A long tradition of economic research has stressed the importance of education in providing the skills and competencies that underpin economic production. But education matters for quality of life independently of its effects on people's earnings and productivity. Education is strongly associated with people's life-evaluations, even after controlling for the higher income it brings. Further, better-educated people typically have better health status, lower unemployment, more social connections and greater engagement in civic and political life. While the available evidence does not always allow conclusions about the directionality of causation between education and these other dimensions of quality of life (e.g., less healthy children may miss school more often), there *is* a consensus that education brings a range of returns (monetary and non-monetary) that benefit both the person investing in the education and the community in which they live. Measuring the size of these wider benefits of education is an important research priority, where progress requires better measures of people's characteristics in a range of domains and surveys that follow the same individual over time.

Available educational indicators cover a broad range of fields. Some refer to inputs (e.g., school enrolment, educational expenditures and school resources), while others refer to throughputs and outputs (e.g., graduation rates, completed years of schooling, standardized test-measures of people's achievements in terms of literacy and numeracy). Which of these indicators is more relevant depends on the stage of a country's development and on the goal of the evaluation exercise. The available indicators highlight large differences across countries, with various educational indicators sometimes highlighting contrasting patterns. Some countries, for example, may combine excellence for students that reach university education with widespread underachievement for a large number of youth, mainly from households at the bottom of the socio-economic ladder. These differences would cancel out in summary measures of education (e.g., mean years of schooling) but have significance for any assessment of quality of life. Within countries, measures of inequality in learning outcomes are especially important for youth at the bottom of the achievement scale who are at risk of poverty or exclusion from well-paid and rewarding jobs in adult life. As education is an important predictor of many dimensions of people's lives, all social surveys should systematically include information on the learning experiences of respondents and of their parents, as well as information on other features shaping the quality of their lives.

Some of the most relevant indicators for assessing the effect of education on quality of life are measures of people's competencies. Several tools have been developed in recent years to measure these in standardized ways, though the tools still have significant limitations. First, and most obviously, not all countries currently implement these surveys. Second, many of these tools were not developed from the perspective of measuring people's capabilities in a broad sense, but for the purpose of assessing educational policies, which typically required focusing on a more narrow set of measurable competencies. Third, existing assessment tools often have a narrow coverage, as schooling is only one of the inputs that lead to knowledge, skills development and improvements in quality of life. Information about the experiences and "soft" competencies acquired by children in their early years remains limited, despite increasing evidence that early-childhood experiences matter for people's learning and quality of life in later years. Measurement tools also remain limited when it comes to comparing the competencies of students in higher education and to assessing workers' experiences in terms of adult education and training (although this will change as new surveys of adult competencies are developed and implemented). As for other features of quality of life, the main problem for indicators in this domain is not the lack of detailed information on education *per se*, but rather the lack of surveys measuring both education and other outcomes that matter for quality of life at the individual level.

Personal Activities

How people spend their time and the nature of their personal activities matters for quality of life, irrespectively of the income generated. The activities that people engage in have effects on their subjective well-being, in terms of both their hedonic experiences (Figure 2.2) and their evaluative judgements. More generally, people do not always "choose" among these activities in the same way as they allocate their budget among various goods, due to a lack of effective alternatives. Further, these choices will generally affect other people within the family and community, with some of these personal activities effectively representing indirect costs to production (e.g., commuting) rather than consumption.

Because of both political demands and the feasibility of providing concrete and comparable measures, the main activities discussed by the Commission have been paid work, unpaid work,

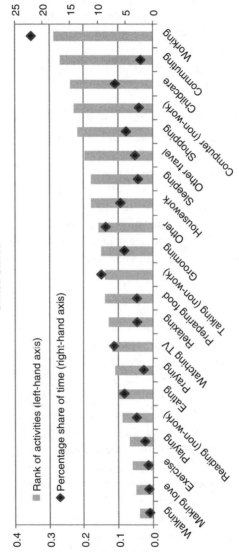

United States

- Rank of activities (left-hand axis)
- Percentage share of time (right-hand axis)

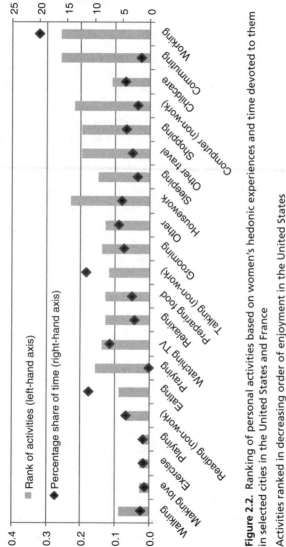

Figure 2.2. Ranking of personal activities based on women's hedonic experiences and time devoted to them in selected cities in the United States and France

Activities ranked in decreasing order of enjoyment in the United States

Note: The ranking of activities is based on information on the proportion of 15-minute intervals in which the hedonic experience of "stress," "sadness" or "pain" exceeded that of "happiness." Data refer to a sample of women in Columbus (Ohio, United States) and Rennes (France), interviewed in 2006 with the *Princeton Affect and Time Survey.*

Source: Krueger, A.B., D. Kahneman, D. Schkade, N. Schwarz and A. Stone (2008), "National Time Accounting: The Currency of Life," NBER, forthcoming in A. B. Kruger (ed.), *Measuring the Subjective Well-Being of Nations: National Accounts of Time Use and Well-Being,* University of Chicago Press, Chicago.

commuting and leisure time. Housing, although not representing an activity *per se*, was also discussed because it provides the setting for a number of personal activities.

- Paid work matters for quality of life partly because it provides identity to people and opportunities to socialize with others. However, not all jobs are equally valuable in this respect. This underscores the importance of collecting more systematic information on the *quality* of paid work, as a number of international organizations have been doing in the context of their ongoing studies of "decent work." Some national surveys provide information on many aspects of decent work, such as non-standard employment, gender gaps in employment and wages, discrimination in the workplace, opportunities for lifelong learning, access to employment for disabled persons, working time and "unsocial hours," the work-life balance, work accidents and physical risks, work intensity, social dialogue and workers' autonomy. Their practical use is, however, limited by small sample sizes and survey differences across countries.
- Unpaid domestic work, such as shopping and the care of children and other household members, is important from the perspective of assessing both the total amount of household services produced and how family chores are distributed between men and women.
- Commuting time is also key to the quality of work, and monitoring it requires information on the number of hours spent travelling to and from work during a specified period, as well as on the accessibility and affordability of transport.
- A long tradition of research has emphasized the importance of leisure-time for quality of life. This research points to the importance of developing indicators of both leisure quantity

(number of hours) and quality (number of episodes, where they took place, presence of other people), as well as of measures of participation in cultural events and of "poor leisure" (such as the share of children who did not take a holiday away from home in the previous year).

- Finally, despite the importance of housing for a variety of social outcomes (such as children's education), no core set of housing indicators currently exists for international comparisons. Remedying this situation would require better information on the number of people who are homeless or living in emergency shelters and on housing quality (e.g., in terms of the local services available and overcrowding).

In several cases, suitable indicators in these various fields already exist, and the challenge is to improve upon what has been achieved in the past. In other areas, however, existing measures remain seriously deficient, and progress requires investment in new statistical capacity. A case in point, cutting across all the personal activities described above, is that of measuring how people spend their time. Time is the natural metric for comparing personal activities and (as argued in chapter 1) an essential input to the construction of satellite household accounts. One priority should be to develop measurement tools grounded on clear definitions and based on surveys with a consistent design that are representative of patterns over a full year and are undertaken with sufficient regularity—all requirements that are rarely met. Ideally, these surveys should cover both the amount of time spent in various activities and the feelings that they produce. This is important, as the same activity can generate different hedonic experiences depending on people's own conditions (e.g., whether they are unemployed or not); this information also matters for assessing inequalities between different groups in society (e.g., by gender).

While these investments in statistical capacity are costly, and compete with other priorities, their pay-off for quality-of-life research is potentially huge.

Political Voice and Governance

Political voice is an integral dimension of the quality of life. Intrinsically, the ability to participate as full citizens, to have a say in the framing of policies, to dissent without fear and to speak up against what one perceives to be wrong are essential freedoms. Instrumentally, political voice can provide a corrective to public policy: it can ensure the accountability of officials and public institutions, reveal what people need and value and call attention to significant deprivations. Political voice also reduces the potential for conflicts and enhances the prospect of building consensus on key issues, with pay-offs for economic efficiency, social equity and inclusiveness in public life.

The opportunities for political voice and the degree of responsiveness of the political system depend on the institutional features of each country, such as the presence of a functioning democracy, universal suffrage, free media and civil society organizations. This also depends on some key aspects of governance, such as legislative guarantees and the rule of law. Legislative guarantees include both constitutional rights and rights provided by general laws that enhance the quality of life of all residents and that reflect the social consensus prevailing in different countries and times. The structure of laws can also affect the investment climate in a country and thus have an impact on market functioning, economic growth, job creation and material welfare. However, to realize their potential, legal guarantees require effective implementation and substantive justice, which depend on how various institutions (e.g., the police, the judiciary and various administrative services) function, whether they are free from corruption, political interference and social prejudice, and whether they can be held accountable for their decisions.

Comparisons based on existing indicators of political voice and governance highlight vast differences between countries, especially between those with a long history of democratic functioning and those that have moved from authoritarian to democratic regimes only more recently and that have not yet established the full range of freedoms and rights. Even in the developed world, however, low trust in public institutions and declining political participation point to a growing gap between how citizens and political elites perceive the functioning of democratic institutions. There are also systematic differences in how different groups exercise political voice, and with respect to fundamental rights and opportunities for civic participation in these countries, especially between citizens and the growing numbers of immigrants.

Indicators of political voice and governance should help to evaluate the functioning of multiparty democracy and universal suffrage, the level of participation in government decisions at the local level and the presence of a free media and various freedoms (e.g., to form and join civil organizations, trade unions and professional bodies, or to participate in civic and social activities). Relevant indicators should cover the rights embedded in constitutions, laws (e.g., that promote civil and criminal justice, equality, inclusion, accountability and affirmative action), international covenants on human rights and basic freedoms, as well as the functioning of the judicial system (e.g., its independence from corruption and political influences, the speed with which it delivers justice and its accessibility to both citizens and residents). Many of these indicators are typically compiled by bodies outside the boundaries of national statistical systems and are based mainly on the opinion of experts. These indicators need to be complemented, and in some cases replaced, by surveys of citizens' own perceptions of how well the political, legal and executive institutions are functioning, the difficulties they face in accessing them and the trust that they place in them. Such surveys also need to capture inequalities in access to these institutions across socio-economic groups.

Social Connections

Social connections improve quality of life in a variety of ways. People with more social connections report higher life-evaluations, as many of the most pleasurable personal activities involve socializing. The benefits of social connections extend to people's health and to the probability of finding a job, as well as to several characteristics of the neighborhood where people live (e.g., the prevalence of crime and the performance of local schools). These social connections are sometimes described as "social capital" to highlight the benefits (direct and indirect) that they bring. As with other types of capital, the externalities stemming from social capital can sometimes be negative: for example, belonging to a group may strengthen a sense of unique personal identity that fuels a climate of violence and confrontation with other groups. This, however, underscores the importance of better analyzing the *nature* of these social connections and the *breadth* of their effects, rather than underestimating their significance. The available evidence suggests that social connections benefit people in the networks, with effects on non-participants that depend on both the nature of the group and the effects being considered.

The drivers of change in people's social connections are not always well understood. Social connections provide services to people (e.g., insurance, security), and the development of both markets and government programs may have reduced the ties of individuals with their community thanks to the provision of alternative arrangements. What is clear is that a decline in these ties may negatively affect people's lives, even when their functions are taken up by market or government alternatives that increase the level of economic activity (such as when the informal surveillance of neighbors is replaced by salaried security guards). To avoid a biased assessment of human well-being, measures of these social connections are therefore needed.

Research on social connections has traditionally relied on proxy measures, such as the number of individual memberships in associations, or the frequency of activities assumed to result from social connections (e.g., altruistic behavior and voter turn-out). However, it is by now accepted that these are not good measures of social connections, and that reliable measures require surveys of peoples' behaviors and activities. In recent years, a number of statistical offices (in the United Kingdom, Australia, Canada, Ireland, the Netherlands and, most recently, the United States) have started surveys that measure various forms of social connections. For example, special modules of the labor-force survey in the United States ask people about their civic and political engagement, their membership and voluntary work in various organizations, their relationship with neighbors and family members and how they get information and news. Similar surveys should be implemented elsewhere, based on questions and protocols that allow valid comparisons across countries and over time. Progress should also be made in measuring additional dimensions of social connections (such as trust in others, social isolation, availability of informal support in case of need, engagement in the workplace and in religious activities, friendship across lines of race, religion and social class) by building on the experience accumulated by some countries in these fields.

Environmental Conditions

Environmental conditions are important not only for sustainability, but also because of their immediate impact on the quality of people's lives. First, they affect human health both directly (through air and water pollution, hazardous substances and noise) and indirectly (through climate change, transformations in the carbon and water cycles, biodiversity loss and natural disasters that affect the health of ecosystems). Secondly, people benefit from environmental services, such as access to clean water and recreation areas, and their rights in this field (including rights to access environmental information) have been increasingly recognized. Third, people value environmental amenities or disamenities, and these valuations affect their actual choices (e.g., of where to live). Lastly, environmental conditions may lead to climatic variations and natural disasters, such as drought and flooding, which damage both the properties and the lives of the affected populations.

Measuring the effects of environmental conditions on people's lives is, however, complex. These effects manifest themselves over different timescales, and their impacts vary depending on people's characteristics (e.g., where they live and work, their metabolic intake). Further, the strength of these relations is often underestimated because of limits in current scientific understanding and in the extent to which various environmental factors have been subject to systemic investigations.

Much progress has been achieved in the last two decades in terms of measuring environmental conditions (through better environmental data, the regular monitoring of indicators and accounting tools), understanding their impacts (e.g., evaluation of related morbidity and mortality, labor productivity, the economic stakes associated with climate change, biodiversity change, damage from disasters) and establishing a right of access to environmental information. A range of environmental indicators can be used to measure human pressure on the environment, the responses from administrations, firms and households to environmental degradation and the actual state of environmental quality.

However, from a quality-of-life perspective, existing indicators remain limited in important respects. For example, emissions indicators refer mainly to the aggregate quantities of various pollutants, rather than to the share of people exposed to dangerous doses. Existing indicators should hence be supplemented in a number of ways, including the regular monitoring of the number of premature deaths from exposure to air pollution; the number of people who lack access to water services and nature, or who are exposed to dangerous levels of noise and pollution; and the damage inflicted by environmental disasters. Survey measures of people's own feelings and evaluations of the environmental conditions of their neighborhood are also needed. Because many of the effects of environmental conditions on quality of life differ across people, these indicators should refer to people grouped according to various classification criteria.

Personal Insecurity

Personal insecurity includes external factors that put at risk the physical integrity of each person: crime, accidents, natural disasters and climate changes are some of the most obvious factors.[5] In extreme cases, these factors can lead to the death of the person involved. While these elements account for only a minority of all deaths, and they are captured by general mortality statistics, one rationale for having specific measures of their frequency is that their effect on people's emotional lives is very different than that of deaths related to medical conditions, as shown by the large impact of bereavement on people's subjective well-being.

Less extreme manifestations of personal insecurity such as crime affect quality of life for a significantly larger number of people, with even larger numbers reporting fear of being a victim of a physical aggression. One of the most remarkable features of reports on subjective fear of crime is how little the fear is related to experienced victimization: countries with a higher share of people reporting fear of crime do not experience a higher victimization while, within countries, older and richer people feel more unsafe than younger and poorer people, despite being less likely to be a victim of crime.

These patterns highlight the importance of developing more regular and reliable measures of personal security to orient public discussion. Victimization surveys are an essential tool to assess the frequency of crime and the fear it generates. Other tools need to be mobilized to assess other threats to personal security, such as domestic violence and violence in countries ravaged by conflict and war.

Economic Insecurity

Uncertainty about the material conditions that may prevail in the future reflects the existence of a variety of risks, in particular for unemployment, illness and old age. The realization of these risks has negative consequences for the quality of life, depending on the severity of the shock, its duration, the stigma associated with it, the risk aversion of each person and the financial implications.

Job loss can lead to economic insecurity when unemployment is recurrent or persistent, when unemployment benefits are low relative to previous earnings or when workers have to accept major cuts in pay, hours or both to find a new job. The consequences of job insecurity are both immediate (as replacement income is typically lower than the earnings on the previous job) and longer term (due to potential losses in wages when the person does find another job). While indicators of these consequences are available, cross-country comparisons are difficult, requiring special investments in this direction. Job insecurity can also be measured by asking workers either to evaluate the security of their present job or to rate their expectation of losing their job in the near future.

The fear of job loss can have negative consequences for the quality of life of the workers (e.g., physical and mental illness, tensions in family life) as well as for firms (e.g., adverse impacts on workers' motivation and productivity, lower identification with corporate objectives) and society as a whole.

Illness can cause economic insecurity both directly and indirectly. For people with no (or only partial) health insurance, medical costs can be devastating; forcing them into debt, to sell their home and assets or to forego treatment at the cost of worse health outcomes in the future. One indicator of illness-related economic insecurity is provided by the share of people without health insurance. However, health insurance can cover different contingencies, and even insured people may incur high out-of-pocket health expenses in the event of illness. To these out-of-pocket health expenses should be added the loss of income that occurs if the person has to stop working and the health (or other) insurance does not provide replacement income.

Old age is not a risk *per se*, but it can still imply economic insecurity due to uncertainty about needs and resources after withdrawal from the labor market. Two types of risk, in particular, are important. The first is the risk of inadequate resources during retirement, due to insufficient future pension payments or to greater needs associated with illness or disability. The second is the risk of volatility in pension payments: while all retirement-income systems are exposed to *some* types of risk, the greater role of the private sector in financing old-age pensions (in the form of both occupational pensions and personal savings) has made it possible to extend the coverage of pension systems in many countries but at the cost of shifting risk from governments and firms towards individuals, thereby increasing their insecurity.

The many factors shaping economic insecurity are reflected in the variety of approaches used to measure them. Some approaches try to quantify the frequency of specific risks, while others look at the consequences of a risk that materializes and at the means available to people to protect themselves from these risks (especially resources provided by social security programs). A comprehensive measure of economic insecurity would ideally account for both the frequency of each risk and its consequences, and some attempts in this direction have been made. A further problem is that of aggregating across the various risks that shape economic insecurity, as the indicators that describe these risks lack a common metric to assess their severity. A final, even more intractable problem is that of accounting for the long-term consequences for quality of life of the various policies used to limit economic insecurity (through their effects on unemployment and labor-force participation).

Cross-Cutting Issues

Most of the measurement challenges described above are specific to each dimension of quality of life, and the Commission has only hinted at some of the work required, leaving it to agencies with expertise in each field to detail concrete action plans. Other challenges, however, are cross-cutting and are unlikely to be picked up through initiatives undertaken separately in each field.[6] Three of these issues deserve special attention.

Inequalities in Quality of Life

The first cross-cutting challenge for quality-of-life indicators is to detail the *inequalities* in individual conditions in the various dimensions of life, rather than just the *average* conditions in each country. To some extent, the failure to account for these inequalities explains the "growing gap"—identified by the French Presidency when establishing the Commission—between the aggregate statistics that dominate policy discussions and people's sentiments about their own conditions.

While established methodologies and data sources can be used to measure inequalities in the distribution of economic resources in a fairly reliable way, the situation is much less satisfactory with respect to the non-monetary dimensions of quality of life. This is especially true given that these inequalities cannot always be described through information on the *size* of the distribution of these features around their mean. For example, differences in the lifespan of people may reflect genetic differences that are randomly distributed in the population: in these circumstances, narrowing the overall distribution of life duration would not make society less "unequal" in any morally compelling way.

The problems, however, go deeper than developing suitable measures. There are many inequalities, and each is significant in itself: this suggests that we should avoid the presumption that one of them (e.g., income) will always encompass all others. At the same time, certain inequalities may be mutually reinforcing. Gender disparities, for example, while pervasive in most countries and groups, are typically much larger for households with lower socio-economic status: in many developing countries, the combined effect of gender and socio-economic status is often to exclude young women in poor households from attending school and getting rewarding jobs, denying them possibilities of self-expression and political voice and exposing them to hazards that put their health at risk. The measurement of some of these inequalities (such as those related to class and socio-economic status) has contributed, over the years, to a wide array of policies and institutions aimed at reducing their intensity and consequences. Other types of inequality, such as between ethnic groups, are more recent (at least in countries that have experienced large waves of immigration) and are set to become more politically salient in the future as immigration continues.

It is critical that these inequalities be assessed in a comprehensive way, by looking at differences in quality of life across people, groups and generations. Further, as people can be classified according to different criteria, each with some relevance for people's lives, inequalities should be measured and documented for a plurality of groups. Appropriate surveys should be developed to assess the complementarities between the various types of inequality and to identify their underlying causes. It is up to the statistical community to regularly feed these analyses with suitable data.

Assessing Links Across Quality-of-Life Dimensions

The second cross-cutting challenge, already alluded to above, is to better assess the *relationship* between the various dimensions of quality of life. Some of the most important policy questions involved relate to how developments in one area (e.g., education) affect developments in others (e.g., health status, political voice and social connections), and how developments in all fields are related to those in income. While some of these relationships, in particular at the individual level, are poorly measured and inadequately understood, ignoring the cumulative effects of multiple disadvantages leads to sub-optimal policies. For example, the loss of quality of life due to being both poor and sick far exceeds the sum of the two separate effects, implying that governments may need to target their interventions more specifically at those who cumulate these disadvantages.

Assessing these links across the various dimensions of quality of life is not easy, as statistical systems continue to be highly segmented across disciplines, with measurement instruments in each field paying only scant attention to developments in other domains. But progress can be achieved by developing information about the "joint distribution" of the most salient features of quality of life (such as hedonic experiences, health status, education, political voice) across all people. While the full development of this information could be achieved only in the distant future, concrete steps in this direction could be accomplished by including in all surveys a few standard questions that allow classifying respondents based on a limited set of characteristics, and that describe their conditions in a broad range of fields. Investment should also be made in developing longitudinal surveys that could allow both controlling for people's personal characteristics and better analyzing the directionality of causation between the different factors shaping life.

Aggregating Across Quality-of-Life Dimensions

The third cross-cutting challenge to quality-of-life research is to *aggregate* the rich array of measures in a parsimonious way. The issue of aggregation is both specific to each feature of quality of life (as in the case of measures that combine mortality and morbidity in the health field) and more general, requiring the valuation and aggregation of the achievements in various domains of life, both for each person and for society as a whole. The search for a scalar measure of quality of life is often perceived as the single most important challenge faced by quality-of-life research. While this emphasis is partly misplaced—the informational content of any aggregate index will always reflect the quality of the measures used in its construction—the demands in this field are strong, and statistical offices should play a role in answering them.

Traditionally, the most common response to this demand for parsimony in quality-of-life research has been to aggregate a number of indicators (suitably selected and scaled) of *average* performance in various fields at the country-level. The best known example of this approach is the Human Development Index. This measure has played (and continues to play) an important communication role, leading to country-rankings that differ significantly from those based on per-capita GDP, especially for some less-developed countries. However, the choices on the weights used to construct this (and other similar) indices reflect value judgments that have controversial implications: for example, adding the *loga-rithm* of per-capita GDP to the *level* of life expectancy (as done by the Human Development Index) implicitly values an additional year of life expectancy in the United States as worth 20 times an additional year of life in India. More fundamentally, being based on country-averages, these measures ignore the significant corre-lations between the various features of quality of life across people, and do not say anything about the distribution of these individual conditions within each country. For example, the scalar index will not change if average performance in each domain remains the same while the accumulation of advantages or disadvantages for the same person across various domains of life changes over time.

Several aggregate measures of quality of life are possible, de-pending on the philosophical perspective taken and the question addressed. Some of these measures are already being used spo-radically (e.g., average levels of life-satisfaction for a country as a whole, and composite indices such as the Human Development Index, which is mainly focused on developing countries) and could be extended through questionnaire-based measures of peo-ple's psychological health, feelings and evaluations, and through consideration of additional dimensions of quality of life. Others could be implemented if national statistical systems made the necessary investment to provide the type of data needed to allow their computation. For example, the U-index, i.e., the proportion of one's time in which the strongest reported feeling is a negative one (see Figure 2.2), requires collecting information on emo-tional experiences during specific episodes through time-use sur-veys. Similarly, methods based on counting the occurrences and severity of various objective features for each person (which is linked to the capability approach), before proceeding to construct country-averages, require information on the joint distribution of various objective features. Finally, the notion of "equivalent income" (which is linked to the fair allocations approach) requires

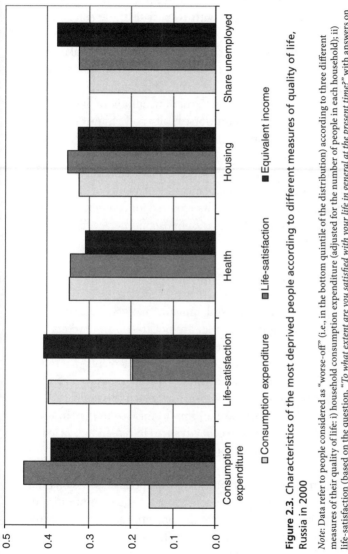

Figure 2.3. Characteristics of the most deprived people according to different measures of quality of life, Russia in 2000

Legend: □ Consumption expenditure ▨ Life-satisfaction ■ Equivalent income

Note: Data refer to people considered as "worse-off" (i.e., in the bottom quintile of the distribution) according to three different measures of their quality of life: i) household consumption expenditure (adjusted for the number of people in each household); ii) life-satisfaction (based on the question, *"To what extent are you satisfied with your life in general at the present time?"* with answers on a five-point scale); and iii) a measure of equivalent income, based on four "functionings" (i.e., self-reported health, employment status, quality of housing, and having incurred wage arrears). For each of these three measures of quality of life, the figure plots the average levels of various factors shaping quality of life among the "worse-off" based on one measure relative to those based on all others.

Source: Fleurbaey M., E. Schokkaert and K. Decancq (2009) "What Good Is Happiness?" CORE Discussion Paper, 2009/17, Université Catholique de Louvain, Belgium. Computations based on data from the *Russia Longitudinal Monitoring Survey*.

information on people's states in various dimensions of quality of life, and on their preferences with respect to these states (for a given reference level in each).

In general, different approaches will lead to distinct scalar measures of quality of life for each country, and to different characteristics of the people classified as "worse-off." For example, in a sample of Russian respondents, people in the bottom quintile of the distribution of equivalent income report worse health and a higher incidence of unemployment compared to people identified as "worse-off" based on either their consumption expenditure or their subjective life-evaluations (Figure 2.3). This suggests that, rather than focusing on constructing a single summary measure of quality of life, statistical systems should provide the data required for computing various aggregate measures according to the philosophic perspective of each user.

Main Messages and Recommendations

Quality of life includes the full range of factors that make life worth living, including those that are not traded in markets and not captured by monetary measures. While some extensions of economic accounting include some additional elements that shape quality of life in conventional money-based measures of economic well-being, there are limits on how much this approach can achieve. Other indicators have an important role to play in measuring social progress, and recent advances in research have led to new and credible measures for at least some aspects of quality of life. These measures, while not replacing conventional economic indicators, provide an opportunity to enrich policy discussions and to inform people's view of the conditions of the communities in which they live; today, they have the potential to move from research to standard statistical practice. The Commission's recommendations in this field can be summarized as follows:

Recommendation 1: Measures of subjective well-being provide key information about people's quality of life. Statistical offices should incorporate questions to capture people's life-evaluations, hedonic experiences and priorities in their own surveys.

Research has shown that it is possible to collect meaningful and reliable data on subjective well-being. Subjective well-being encompasses different aspects (cognitive evaluations of one's life, positive emotions such as joy and pride and negative emotions such as pain and worry): each of them should be measured separately to derive a more comprehensive appreciation of people's lives. Quantitative measures of these subjective aspects hold the promise of delivering not just a good measure of quality of life *per se*, but also a better understanding of its determinants, reaching beyond people's income and material conditions. Despite the persistence of many unresolved issues, these subjective measures provide important information about quality of life. Because of this, the types of questions that have proved their value within small-scale, unofficial surveys should be included in larger-scale surveys undertaken by official statistical offices.

Recommendation 2: Quality of life also depends on people's objective conditions and opportunities. Steps should be taken to improve measures of people's health, education, personal activities, political voice, social connections, environmental conditions and security.

The information relevant to valuing quality of life goes beyond people's self-reports and perceptions to include measures of their functionings and freedoms. While the precise list of these features inevitably rests on value judgments, there is a consensus that quality of life depends on people's health and education, their everyday activities (which include the right to a decent job and housing), their participation in the political process, the social and natural environment in which they live and the factors shaping their personal and economic security. Measuring all these features requires both objective and subjective data. The challenge in all these fields is to improve upon what has already been achieved, to identify gaps in available information, and to invest in statistical capacity in areas (such as time-use) where available indicators remain deficient.

Recommendation 3: Quality-of-life indicators in all the dimensions they cover should assess inequalities in a comprehensive way.
Inequalities in human conditions are integral to any assessment of quality of life across countries and the way that it is developing over time. Each dimension of quality of life requires appropriate measures of inequality, with each of these measures being significant in itself and none claiming absolute priority over others. Inequalities should be assessed across people, socio-economic groups and generations, with special attention to inequalities that have arisen more recently, such as those linked to immigration.

Recommendation 4: Surveys should be designed to assess the links between various quality-of-life domains for each person, and this information should be used when designing policies in various fields.
It is critical to address questions about how developments in one domain of quality of life affect other domains, and how developments in all the various fields are related to income. This is important because the consequences for quality of life of having multiple disadvantages far exceed the sum of their individual effects. Developing measures of these cumulative effects requires information on the "joint distribution" of the most salient features of quality of life across everyone in a country through dedicated surveys. Steps in this direction could also be taken by including in all surveys some standard questions that allow classifying respondents based on a limited set of characteristics. When designing policies in specific fields, indicators pertaining to different quality-of-life dimensions should be considered jointly, to address the interactions between

dimensions and the needs of people who are disadvantaged in several domains.

Recommendation 5: Statistical offices should provide the information needed to aggregate across quality-of-life dimensions, allowing the construction of different scalar indices.

While assessing quality of life requires a plurality of indicators, there are strong demands to develop a single scalar measure. Several scalar measures of quality of life are possible, depending on the question addressed and the approach taken. Some of these measures are already being used, such as average levels of life-satisfaction for a country as a whole, or composite indices that aggregate averages across domains, such as the Human Development Index. Others could be implemented if national statistical systems made the necessary investment to provide the data required for their computation. These include measures of the proportion of one's time in which the strongest reported feeling is a negative one, measures based on counting the occurrence and severity of various objective features of people's lives and (equivalent-income) measures based on people's states and preferences.

3

SUSTAINABLE DEVELOPMENT
AND ENVIRONMENT[7]

Introduction

The first two chapters have dealt extensively with the measurement of current well-being, either along dimensions that can be summed up in monetary units (chapter 1), or along dimensions that are less amenable to conversion into monetary units (chapter 2).

The sustainability issue that is raised by this last chapter is of a different nature. Sustainability poses the challenge of determining whether we can hope to see the current level of well-being at least maintained for future periods or future generations, or whether the most likely scenario is that it will decline. It is no longer a question of measuring the present, but of predicting the future, and this prospective dimension multiplies the difficulties already encountered in the first two chapters.

Despite these difficulties, many proposals have been made for measuring sustainability in quantitative terms, stemming from seminal work such as Nordhaus and Tobin's "sustainable measure of economic welfare" in the 1970s, or following the strong impulse given by the Brundtland Report in 1987 and the Rio Summit at the turn of the 1990s. The present chapter will start with a short review of these proposals. We shall see that many of them fail to distinguish clearly between the measurement of current well-being and the assessment of its sustainability. To put it very simply, many proposals try to cover all three dimensions examined by the three subgroups of the Commission, and sometimes try to sum them up in a single number. This is not the way the Commission has structured its approach, and with good reason. We firmly believe that sustainability deserves separate measurement, and we shall focus in this chapter on the sustainability issue *stricto sensu*.

Such a restriction allows focusing on what the literature calls a "wealth" or "stock-based" approach to sustainability. The idea is the following: the well-being of future generations compared to ours will depend on what resources we pass on to them. Many different forms of resources are involved here. Future well-being will depend upon the magnitude of the stocks of exhaustible resources that we leave to the next generations. It will depend also on how well we maintain the quantity and quality of all the other renewable natural resources that are necessary for life. From a more economic point of view, it will also depend upon how much physical capital— machines and buildings—we pass on, and how much we devote to the constitution of the human capital of future generations, essentially through expenditure on education and research. And it also depends upon the quality of the institutions that we transmit to them, which is still another form of "capital" that is crucial for maintaining a properly functioning human society.

How can we measure whether enough of these assets will be left or accumulated for future generations? In other words, when can we say that we are currently living above our means? In particular, is there any reasonable hope of being able to characterize this with one simple number that could play the role for sustainability that GDP has long played for the measurement of economic performance? One reason for such a quest would be to avoid the multiplication of competing numbers. However, if we want to accomplish this, we need to convert all the stocks of resources passed on to future generations into a common metric, be it monetary or not.

We shall discuss in some detail why such a goal seems overly ambitious. The aggregation of heterogeneous items seems possible up to a point for physical and human capital or some natural resources that are traded on markets. But the task appears much more complicated for most natural assets, due to the lack of relevant market prices and to the many uncertainties concerning the way these natural assets will interact with other dimensions of sustainability in the future. This will lead us to suggest a pragmatic approach that combines a monetary indicator, which could send us reasonable signals about economic sustainability, and a set of physical indicators devoted to environmental issues. We provide some examples of such physical indicators, yet, in the end, the choice of the most relevant ones must be left to specialists from other fields, before submission to the public debate.

Taking Stock

Providing a brief summary of the very abundant literature that has been devoted to the measurement of sustainability or durable development is not an easy task. We will use an imperfect but simple typology that distinguishes (1) large and eclectic dashboards, (2) composite indices, (3) indices that consist of correcting GDP in a more or less extensive way and (4) indices that essentially focus on measuring how far we currently "overconsume" our resources. This last category is itself heterogeneous, since we shall include in it indices as different as the ecological footprint and adjusted net savings, which, as we shall see, convey very different messages.

Dashboards or Sets of Indicators

Dashboards or sets of indicators are one widespread approach to the general question of sustainable development. This approach involves gathering and ordering a series of indicators that bear a direct or indirect relationship to socio-economic progress and its durability. In the last couple of decades, international organizations have played a major role in the emergence of sustainability dashboards, with the United Nations playing a prominent role. In particular, the 1992 Rio Summit adopted Agenda 21, whose 40th chapter invites the signatory countries to develop quantitative information about their actions and accomplishments.

Other international initiatives to build sustainable development dashboards have been taken by the OECD and Eurostat, following the European Council's adoption of its own Sustainable Development Strategy in 2001. The current version of this dashboard includes 11 indicators for level 1 (Table 3.1), 33 indicators for level 2 and 78 indicators for level 3, with the level 2 and 3 indicators covering 29 sub-themes. Similar national initiatives have accompanied this general movement, albeit in a somewhat scattered way. Local initiatives have also mushroomed over the last decade, some based on the initial impetus from Agenda 21.

Table 3.1. Reviewed List of European Sustainable Development Indicators (level 1)

Theme	Level 1 indicators
1. Socio-economic development	Growth rate of GDP per inhabitant
2. Sustainable consumption and production	Resource productivity
3. Social inclusion	At-risk-of-poverty rate after social transfers
4. Demographic changes	Employment rate of older workers
5. Public health	Healthy life years and life expectancy at birth
6. Sustainable development	Total greenhouse gas emissions
	Consumption of renewables
7. Sustainable transport	Energy consumption of transport
8. Natural resources	Common bird index
	Fish catches outside safe biological limits
9. Global partnership	Official Development Assistance (ODA)

Source: Eurostat, 2007 (http://epp.eurostat.ec.europa.eu/cache/ITY_OFFPUB/KS-77-07-115/EN/KS-77-07-115-EN.PDF).

For the user, the most striking feature of this very abundant literature is the extreme variety of the indicators proposed. Some are very comprehensive—GDP growth retains its place, and is even the first indicator in the European Dashboard—while others are much more specific, such as the percentage of smokers in the population. Some pertain to outcomes, others to instruments. Some can easily be related both to development *and* to sustainability—literacy performance matters for both current well-being and future growth—but others pertain only either to current development or to long-run sustainability. There are even some items whose link with both dimensions is questionable or at least of indeterminate sign: is a high fertility rate a good thing for sustainability? Maybe yes for the sustainability of pensions, but maybe not for environmental sustainability. And is it always a signal of good economic performance? This probably depends on what we consider "high" or "low" in terms of fertility.

These dashboards are useful in at least two respects. First, they are an initial step in any analysis of sustainability, which by its nature is highly complex and therefore necessitates an effort at establishing a list of relevant variables and encouraging national and international statistical offices to improve the measurement of these indicators. The second one is related to the distinction between "weak" and "strong" sustainability. The "weak" approach to sustainability considers that good performance in some dimensions can compensate for low performance in others. This allows a global assessment of sustainability using mono-dimensional indices. The "strong" approach argues that sustainability requires separately maintaining the quantity or quality of many different environmental items. Following this up therefore requires large sets of separate statistics, each pertaining to one particular subdomain of global sustainability.

Dashboards nevertheless suffer because of their heterogeneity, at least in the case of very large and eclectic ones, and most lack indications about causal links, their relationship to sustainability and/or hierarchies among the indicators used. Further, as communications instruments, one frequent criticism is that they lack what has made GDP a success: the powerful attraction of a single headline figure allowing simple comparisons of socioeconomic performance over time or across countries.

Composite Indices

Composite indices are one way to circumvent the problem raised by the richness of dashboards and to synthesize the abundant and purportedly relevant information into a single number. The technical report reviews a few of these.

For example, Osberg and Sharpe's Index of Economic Well-Being is a composite indicator that simultaneously covers current prosperity (based on measures of consumption), sustainable accumulation and social topics (reduction in inequalities and protection against "social" risks). Environmental issues are addressed by considering the costs of CO_2 emissions per capita. Consumption flows and wealth accumulation (defined broadly to include R&D stocks, a proxy for human capital and the costs of CO_2 emissions) are evaluated according to national accounts methodology. Each dimension is normalized through linear scaling (nine OECD countries) and aggregation relies on equal weighting. But at this stage the "green" dimension of this index is still secondary.

Other examples focus more specifically on the green dimension, such as the "Environmental Sustainability Index" (ESI) and the "Environmental Performance Index" (EPI). The ESI covers 5 domains: environmental systems (their global health status), environmental stress (anthropogenic pressure on the environmental systems), human vulnerability (exposure of inhabitants to environmental disturbances), social and institutional capacity (their capacity to foster effective responses to environmental challenges) and global stewardship (cooperation with other countries in the management of common environmental problems). It uses 76 variables to cover these 5 domains. There are, for instance, standard indicators for air and water quality (e.g., SO_2 and NO_x), health parameters (e.g., infant death rate from respiratory diseases), environmental governance (e.g., local Agenda 21 initiatives per million people), etc. The EPI is a reduced form of the ESI, based on 16 indicators (outcomes), and is more policy-oriented.

The messages derived from this kind of index are ambiguous. The global ranking of countries has some sense, but it is often considered to present an overly optimistic view of developed countries' contributions to environmental problems. Problems also arise between developed countries. For instance, the index shows a very narrow gap between the United States and France, despite strong differences in terms of their CO_2 emissions. In fact, the index essentially informs us about a mix of current environmental quality, of pressure on resources and of the intensity of environmental policy, but not about whether a country is actually on a sustainable path: no threshold value can be defined on either side of which we would be able to say that a country is or is not on a sustainable path.

On the whole, these composite indicators are better regarded as invitations to look more closely at the various components that underlie them. This kind of function of composite indicators has often been put forward as one of their main *raisons d'être*. But this is not reason enough to retain them as measures of sustainability *stricto sensu* which could secure the same standing as GDP or other accounting concepts. There are two reasons for this. First, as with large dashboards, there is the lack of a well-defined notion of what sustainability means. The second is a general criticism that is frequently addressed at composite indicators, i.e., the arbitrary character of the procedures used to weight their various components. These aggregation procedures are sometimes presented as superior to the monetary aggregations that are used to build most economic indices, because they are not linked to any form of market valuation. Indeed, and we shall come back to this point several times, there are many reasons why market values cannot be trusted when addressing sustainability issues, and more specifically their environmental component. But monetary or not, an aggregation procedure always means putting relative values on the items that are introduced in the index. In the case of composite sustainability indicators, we have little understanding of the arguments for putting one relative value or another on all the different variables that matter for sustainability. The problem is not that these weighting procedures are hidden, non-transparent or non-replicable—they are often very explicitly presented by the authors of the indices, and this is one of the strengths of this literature. The problem is rather that their normative implications are seldom made explicit or justified.

Adjusted GDPs

Other candidates for the measurement of sustainability are those that restart from the conventional notion of GDP but try to systematically augment or correct it using elements that standard GDP does not take into account and that matter for sustainability.

Nordhaus and Tobin's sustainable measure of economic welfare (SMEW) may be regarded as the common ancestor to this strand. They provided two indicators. The first was a measure of economic welfare (MEW) obtained by subtracting from total private consumption a number of components that do not contribute positively to welfare (such as commuting and legal services) and by adding monetary estimates of activities that do contribute positively to welfare (such as leisure and work at home). The second step consisted in converting the MEW into the SMEW by taking into account changes in total wealth. The SMEW measures the level of MEW that is compatible with preserving the capital stock. To convert the MEW into the SMEW, Nordhaus and Tobin used an estimate of total public and private wealth, including reproducible capital, non-reproducible capital (limited to land and net foreign assets), educational capital (based on the cumulated cost of years spent in education by people belonging to the labor force) and health capital, based on a permanent inventory method with a depreciation rate of 20% per year. But they did not in the end include estimates of environmental damage or natural resource depletion.

Two strands have developed from this seminal contribution. The first has tried to enrich Nordhaus and Tobin's approach, sometimes deviating increasingly from the criterion of accounting consistency. Examples include the Index of Sustainable Economic Welfare (ISEW) and the Genuine Progress Indicator (GPI). These indicators deduct some evaluations of the costs of water, air and noise pollution from consumption and also try to account for the loss of wetlands, farmland and primary forests, and for other natural resource depletion, and for CO_2 damage and ozone depletion. Natural resources depletion is valued by measuring the investment necessary to generate a perpetual equivalent stream of renewable substitutes.

In all countries for which both ISEW and GPI are available, their values are very similar and at some point in time start diverging from GDP. This has led some authors to put forward a so-called "threshold" hypothesis, according to which GDP and welfare move in the same direction up to a certain point, beyond which the continuation of GDP growth does not allow any further improvement in well-being. In other words, according to such indicators, sustainability is already far behind us, and we have already entered a phase of decline.

The other strand is more firmly integrated into the realm of national accounting. It is based on the so-called System of Environmental Economic Accounting (SEEA), a satellite account of the Standard National Accounts (SNA). The SEEA brings together economic and environmental information in a common framework to measure the contribution of the environment to the economy and the impact of the economy on the environment. The UN Committee of Experts on Environmental-Economic Accounting (UNCEEA), created in 2005, is now looking to mainstream environmental economic accounting, to elevate the SEEA to an international statistical standard by 2010 and to advance SEEA implementation in countries.

The SEEA comprises four categories of accounts. The first considers purely physical data related to flows of materials (materials drawn into the economy and residuals produced as waste) and energy and marshals them as far as possible according to the SNA accounting structure. The second category of accounts takes those elements of the existing SNA that are relevant to the good management of the environment and makes the environment-related transactions more explicit. The third category of accounts comprises accounts for environmental assets measured in physical and monetary terms (timber stock accounts, for instance).

These first three categories of the SEEA are vital building blocks for any form of sustainability indicator. But what is at stake here is the fourth and last category of SEEA accounts, which deals with how the existing SNA might be adjusted to account (exclusively in monetary terms) for the impact of the economy on the environment. Three sorts of adjustments are considered: those relating to resource depletion, those concerning so-called defensive expenditures (protection expenditures being the most emblematic ones) and those relating to environmental degradation.

It is these environmental adjustments to existing SNA aggregates that are better known under the rather loose expression of

"Green GDP," which is an extension of the concept of net domestic product. Indeed, just as GDP (Gross) is turned into NDP (Net) by accounting for the consumption of fixed capital (depreciation of produced capital), the idea is that it would be meaningful to compute an "ea-NDP" (environmentally-adjusted) that takes into account the consumption of natural capital. The latter would comprise resource depletion (the overuse of environmental assets as inputs to the production process) and environmental degradation (the value of the decline in the quality of a resource, roughly speaking).

Green GDP and ea-NDP remain, however, the most controversial outcomes of the SEEA, and as such are less implemented by statistical offices, because of the many problems that are raised by these two concepts. Valuing environmental inputs into the economic system is the (relatively) easier step. Since these inputs are incorporated into products that are sold in the marketplace, it is possible (in principle) to use direct means to assign a value for them based on market principles. In contrast, as pollution emissions are outputs, there is no direct way to assign a value to them. All the indirect methods of valuation will depend to some extent on "what if" scenarios. Thus, translating valuations of degradation into adjustments to macro-economic aggregates takes us beyond the realm of *ex-post accounting* into a much more hypothetical situation. The very speculative nature of this sort of accounting explains the great discomfort and strong resistance among many accountants to this practice.

But there is a more fundamental problem with Green GDP, which also applies to Nordhaus and Tobin's SMEW and to the ISEW/GNI indices. None of these measures characterize sustainability *per se*. Green GDP just charges GDP for the depletion of or damage to environmental resources. This is only one part of the answer to the question of sustainability. What we ultimately need is an assessment of how far we are from these sustainable targets.

In other words, what we need are measures of *overconsumption* or, to put in dual terms, of *underinvestment*. This is precisely what our last category of indicators purports to do.

Indicators Focusing on Overconsumption or Underinvestment

Under this heading, we group all kinds of indicators that address the issue of sustainability in terms of overconsumption, underinvestment or excessive pressure on resources. Though such indicators tend to be presented in flow terms, they are built upon the assumption that some stocks that are relevant for sustainability correspond to the measured flows, i.e., stocks that are being transmitted to future generations and determine their opportunity sets. As with GDP and other aggregates, trying to perform this task with a single number requires the choice of a metric and an explicit aggregation procedure for these stocks and their variations.

Adjusted Net Savings (ANS)

Adjusted net savings (also known as genuine savings or genuine investment) is a sustainability indicator that builds on the concepts of green national accounts but reformulates these concepts in terms of stock or wealth rather than flows of income or consumption. The theoretical background is the idea that sustainability requires the maintenance of a constant stock of "extended wealth," which is not limited to natural resources but also includes physical, productive capital, as measured in traditional national accounts, and human capital. Net adjusted savings is taken to be the change in this total wealth over a given time period, such as a year. Such a concept clearly appears to be the relevant economic counterpart of the notion of sustainability, in that it includes not only natural resources but also (in principle at least) those other ingredients necessary to provide future generations an opportunity set that is at least as large as what is currently available to living generations.

Empirically, adjusted net savings are derived from standard national accounting measures of gross national savings by making four types of adjustment. First, estimates of the capital consumption of produced assets are deducted to obtain net national savings. Second, current expenditures on education are added to net domestic savings as an appropriate value for investment in human capital (in standard national accounting these expenditures are treated as consumption). Third, estimates of the depletion of a variety of natural resources are deducted to reflect the decline in asset values associated with their extraction and harvest. Estimates of resource depletion are based on the calculation of resource rents. An economic rent represents the "excess" return to a given factor of production. Rents are derived by taking the difference between world prices and the average unit extraction or harvest cost (including a "normal" return on capital). Finally, global pollution damages from carbon dioxide emissions are deducted.[8] Negative adjusted net savings rates imply that "extended wealth" is in decline, and as such provide a warning of non-sustainability.

How does this indicator compare with standard measures of saving and investment in national accounts? World Bank-computed ANS for developed countries such as France and the United States shows that changes over time are almost exclusively driven by gross savings, while the gap in levels between ANS and gross savings is due mostly to capital consumption and human capital accumulation whereas, according to the index, natural capital changes play only a relatively marginal role. Moreover, the ANS figures show that most developed countries are on a sustainable path, while many emerging or developing countries are not. In particular, according to this measure most natural resource-exporting countries are on a non-sustainable path (Figure 3.1).

This kind of approach appeals to many economists, as it is grounded on an explicit theoretical framework. However, the current methodology underlying empirical calculations has well-known shortcomings: the relevance of the ANS approach crucially depends on *what* is counted (the different forms of capital passed on to future generations), namely, what is included in "extended wealth," and on the *price* used to count and aggregate in a context of imperfect or indeed non-existent valuation by markets—the problem that we already mentioned when discussing the implicit prices used by composite indicators.

Indeed, a major shortcoming of ANS estimates is that the adjustment for environmental degradation is only limited to a restricted set of pollutants, the most significant one being carbon dioxide emissions. The authors acknowledge that the calculations do not include other important sources of environmental degradation, such as underground water depletion, unsustainable fisheries, soil degradation and *a fortiori* biodiversity loss.

For those natural assets that are taken into account, pricing techniques remain the major issue. For exhaustible resources, the World Bank's estimates of ANS rely on current prices. In theory, the use of market prices to evaluate flows and stocks is warranted only in a context of perfect markets, which is clearly not the case in reality, and especially not for natural resources, where externalities and uncertainties are paramount. Further, market prices for fossil energy sources and other minerals have tended, in recent years, to fluctuate widely, causing significant swings in measures of ANS based on current market prices and this has very strongly reduced the practical relevance of the ANS for concerned countries.

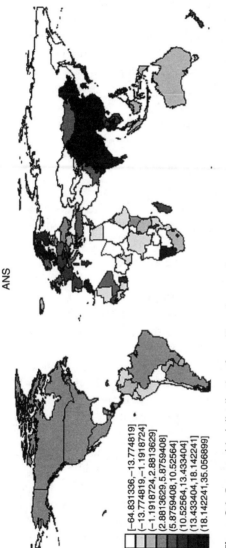

ANS

Figure 3.1. Geographical distribution for adjusted net savings

Source: World Bank, data for 2006.

Reading: Countries are ranked from the most unsustainable (in white) to the most sustainable (in dark). Non-sustainability can be due either to the overextraction of exhaustible resources or to low investment in human and physical capital. The frontiers of countries with missing values are not represented.

Legend:

[−64.831336,−13.774819]
(−13.774819,−1.1918724]
(−1.1918724,2.8813629]
(2.8813629,5.8759408]
(5.8759408,10.52564]
(10.52564,13.433404]
(13.433404,18.142241]
(18.142241,35.056899]

As for pricing environmental degradation, things turn out to be even trickier because of the absence of any market valuation that could be used as a starting point: in theory, we must evaluate so-called "accounting prices" by modeling the long-term consequences of given changes in environmental capital and how they impact future well-being. But practical implementation raises considerable problems. Under the current state of the art, the prices used to value carbon emissions in existing estimates of ANS are not able to give it any significant role in the global assessment of sustainability, and this casts doubts on the usefulness of the indicator as a guide for policy.

Finally, by computing ANS per country we miss the global nature of sustainability. Indeed, one may feel uneasy when faced with the message conveyed by ANS about resource-exporting countries (e.g., oil). In these countries, from the ANS perspective, non-sustainability stems from an insufficient rate of reinvestment of the income generated by the exploitation of the natural resource: "overconsumption" by importing countries is not an issue at all. Developed countries, which are generally less endowed with natural resources but richer in human and physical capital than developing ones, would then appear unduly sustainable. As a consequence, some authors have argued in favor of imputing the consumption of exhaustible resources to their final consumers, i.e., the importing countries. If scarcities were fully reflected in the prices at which exhaustible resources are sold on international markets, it is true that there would be no reason for making such a correction. However, when prices are non-competitive, the importing country pays less for its imports than would be required; it will have a responsibility in global non-sustainability that is not captured by the money-value of its imports. Low prices allow such countries to overconsume and to transfer the long-term costs of this overconsumption to the exporting countries.

Footprints

Although apparently quite different from "extended wealth" notions, various attempts at measuring sustainability through the use of "footprints" are also inspired by the general approach of comparing current flows of consumption and their effects on certain dimensions of the environment with an existing stock. In this sense, they may also be regarded as "wealth" measures. However, the focus is exclusively on natural capital, and the valuation convention differs from the ANS one in that no market prices are explicitly used.

The Ecological Footprint (hereafter EF) measures how much of the regenerative capacity of the biosphere is used up by human activities (consumption). It does so by calculating the amount of biologically productive land and water area required to support a given population at its current level of consumption. A country's footprint (demand side) is the total area required to produce the food, fiber and timber that it consumes, absorb the waste that it generates and provide space for its infrastructure (built-up areas). On the supply side, biocapacity is the productive capacity of the biosphere and its ability to provide a flux of biological resources and services useful to humankind.

The results are well-known and rather striking: since the mid-1980s, humanity's footprint has been larger than the planet's carrying capacity, and in 2003 humanity's total footprint exceeded the Earth's biocapacity by approximately 25 percent. While 1.8 global hectares per person are available worldwide, Europeans use 4.9 global hectares per person and North Americans use twice that amount, that is, much more than the actual biocapacity of those two geographical zones (Figure 3.2).

This indicator shares with accounting approaches the idea of reducing heterogeneous elements to one common measurement

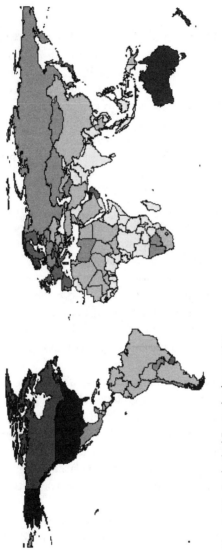

Figure 3.2. Ecological Footprint by country

Source: Global Footprint Network, data for year 2005.

Reading: Dark areas correspond to countries with the highest values for the Ecological Footprint, i.e., with the highest contributions to worldwide unsustainability. Countries with missing values are not represented.

unit (the global hectare, e.g., one hectare with productivity equal to the average productivity of the 11.2 billion bioproductive hectares on Earth). It assumes that different forms of natural capital are substitutable and that different natural capital goods are additive in terms of land area, but strongly stands against weak sustainability assumptions. In fact, this indicator gives no role to savings and capital accumulation: any positive ecological surplus (biocapacity that exceeds the EF) does not entail an increase in some natural capital stock, and hence an improvement in future productive capacity. *A fortiori*, saving and accumulating manufactured or human capital does not help sustainability. On the other hand, one must observe that the indicator ignores the threat to sustainability resulting from the depletion of non-renewable resources (e.g., oil): the consequences for sustainability are treated only from the waste assimilation (implied CO_2 emissions) point of view rather than from an analysis based on depletion dynamics.

The results are also problematic for measuring a country's own sustainability, because of the substantial anti-trade bias inherent in the EF methodology. The fact that densely populated (low biocapacity) countries like the Netherlands have ecological deficits, whilst sparsely populated (high biocapacity) countries like Finland enjoy surpluses can be seen as part of a normal situation where trade is mutually beneficial, rather than an indicator of non-sustainability. Indeed, recent research has tended to move away from comparing a country's EF with its *own* biocapacity, and to propose instead to divide all countries' EFs by *global* biocapacity. By doing this, one is acknowledging that EFs are not measures of a country's own sustainability but of its contribution to global non-sustainability.

Overall, this means that the EF could at best be an indicator of instantaneous non-sustainability *at the worldwide level*. EFs for countries should be used as indicators of inequality in the exploitation of natural resources and interdependencies between geographical areas. Moreover, even the worldwide ecological deficit emphasized by the EF may not convey the message it is said to. Indeed, one can show that the worldwide imbalance is mostly driven by CO_2 emissions, expressed in hectares of forest needed for storage. By definition, the worldwide demand placed on cropland, built-up land and pasture cannot exceed world biocapacity.

As a result, less-encompassing but more-rigorously-defined footprints, such as the Carbon Footprint (CF), would seem better-suited, insofar as they are more clearly physical measures of stocks that do not rely on specific assumptions about productivity or an equivalence factor. As far as communications is concerned, such an indicator is just as capable of sending strong messages in terms of the overutilization of the planet's capacity for absorption. The CF also has the interesting feature of being computable at any level of disaggregation. This makes it a powerful instrument for monitoring the behavior of individual actors.

Quantifying Sustainability in a Consensual Way: What Are the Main Stumbling Blocks?

Let's summarize the main messages so far. The previous section has shown the large number of existing attempts to quantify sustainability. This abundance of measures is a serious drawback insofar as different synthetic indicators convey widely divergent messages. This leads to a great deal of confusion among statisticians and policymakers. It urges a return to the fundamental questions: What do we want to measure exactly? What are the real obstacles to doing so with a single headline measure?

What Do We Want to Measure?

Since the Brundtland Report, the notion of sustainable development has expanded to become an all-encompassing concept that absorbs every dimension of present and future economic, social and environmental well-being. Such an ambition is justified, but it covers all the domains considered by the three subgroups of the Commission. The mandate of our environment/sustainability subgroup was narrower than that: it concentrated on the "sustainable" component of "sustainable development." This question of durability can be expressed in the following terms: assuming we have been able to assess what is the current level of well-being, the question is whether the continuation of present trends does or does not allow it to be maintained.

It seems reasonable to separate the two notions of current well-being and of its sustainability, because the two questions are interesting in themselves. This provides a first guide for sorting out the many different approaches reviewed in the first half of this chapter.

- The extensive dashboards of sustainable development effectively conflate the measurement of current well-being and the measurement of its sustainability. This is not to say that dashboards are of no use. Quite the contrary: our final conclusion will be that a unidimensional view of sustainability certainly remains out of reach. But we do want to end up with a limited number of indicators—a "micro" dashboard—and one that is specifically dedicated to the sustainability issue, based on a clear notion of what sustainability means.

- Composite indicators raise similar problems, with the additional complication that the way in which various items are weighted is arbitrary, with consequences that are seldom made explicit.

- Measures of a *sustainable standard of living*, such as the Green GDP, are also insufficient for assessing sustainability. The proximity that such a sustainability indicator would necessarily have with standard GDP could be a source of confusion. If there are two GDP indicators, which one should we use in which context? What conclusion would we draw from the fact that a given country's Green GDP is x% or y% of its GDP defined in standard terms? Does this necessarily imply that this country is on an unsustainable path?

In fact, Green GDP focuses on only one side of the problem, i.e., the measurement of what can be consumed every year without environmental impoverishment. This does not tell us whether we are on a sustainable path. If we want to measure sustainability, what is required is a *comparison* between this concept of genuine production and current consumption. All this makes the appropriate sustainability index more akin to a concept of net investment or disinvestment, and this is precisely the route that extended wealth or ANS exemplifies, but which is also implicitly followed by footprint indicators that are more specifically focused on the renewal or depletion of environmental assets. The argument goes as follows: the capacity of future generations to have standards of well-being at least equal to ours depends upon our passing them sufficient amounts of all the assets that matter for well-being. If we denote by "W" the "extended wealth" index used to quantify this stock of re sources, measuring sustainability amounts to testing whether this global stock or some of its components evolve positively or negatively, i.e., computing its or their current rates of change, dW or dW_i. If negative, this means that downward adjustments in consumption or well-being will be required sooner or later. This is exactly what one should understand by "non-sustainability."

In our view, such a formulation of the sustainability issue has the potential to provide the common language necessary for constructive debates between people from very different perspectives. To take just one example, it fully answers one of the longstanding objections made to GDP by environmentalists, i.e., the fact that ecological catastrophes can increase GDP through their implied impact on economic activity. In an extended wealth approach, an ecological catastrophe is registered as a destruction of capital. This accounts for the fact that it deteriorates sustainability by decreasing the resources available for generating future well-being. This outcome can be avoided only if some action is taken to repair the damage, with these actions being counted as positive investment.

Summarizing Sustainability in One Number: Is It Realistic?

Now, we have seen that both ANS and footprint evaluations are subject to many objections and can be considered, at best, as proxies of what would be genuine indices of changes in extended wealth or its components. Returning to fundamentals means asking precisely what would be required to measure the above-mentioned dW indices in a satisfactory way. Assuming away the measurement problems at first, we have to be more specific about several concepts: What is to be sustained? How do the various assets that will be passed on to future generations affect this measure of well-being? And how should they be weighted against each other?

It is clearly this last question that is more problematic and tends to crystallize opposition between the proponents of monetary indicators and physical indicators. Is there actually some reasonable prospect of evaluating everything in money units, or should we accept that this is possible only up to a certain point?

If all assets were traded on perfect markets by perfectly forward-looking agents fully taking into account the welfare of future generations, one could argue that their current prices reflect the discounted streams of their future contributions to future well-being. But many assets are not traded at all, and even for those that are it is unlikely that current prices fully reflect this future-oriented dimension, due to market imperfections, myopia and uncertainty. This implies that a true measure of sustainability requires a dW index in which assets are valued not at market prices, but rather using imputed "accounting prices" based on some objective physical or economic modeling of how future damage to the environment will affect well-being, just as it requires an exact evaluation of how current additions to the stock of human or physical capital are likely to improve or help maintain well-being in the future.

Recent research has clarified the requisites of such an exercise. One is a full set of economic and physical projection of how initial conditions determine the future joint path of economic, social and environmental variables. Another is the *a priori* definition of how this path translates in terms of well-being at all future dates, i.e., the knowledge of the social utility function, generally formalized as a discounted sum of well-being over all future periods.

Equipped with such instruments, it should be possible to derive sustainability indices that have the properties that one would expect, i.e., a capacity to anticipate future declines in well-being below its current level. Some simulations proposed in the technical report illustrate certain aspects of this capacity. First of all, this sustainability index is the best suited for sending correct forewarnings to countries that are on unsustainable paths because of an insufficient rate of accumulation or of renewal of their produced capital, be it human or physical. And this is of course an important property: even if environmental issues are of considerable importance, we cannot ignore these other dimensions of sustainability.

Second, such an indicator is inconsistent with the "strong" view of non-sustainability (i.e., problems arising from the depreciation of environmental assets that are essential to human well-being or even survival) only when it relies on fixed price levels for natural and non-natural assets. But if we were able to derive this index from a physical-economic model predicting future interactions between the economy and the environment in a reliable way, then this index would send us correct forewarnings of non-sustainability, through strong increases in the relative accounting or "imputed" prices of these critical natural assets.

But the problem is with those "ifs." This construction remains fully theoretical. It shows us at best the direction in which index builders could try to go. It can also be used as a tool for emphasizing the many obstacles to the building of a comprehensive index and the need for more pragmatic second-best solutions.

Technological Uncertainties Argue in Favor of a More Hybrid Approach

Measuring sustainability with a single dW index can work only under two strong assumptions: one is that future eco-environmental developments can be predicted perfectly, and the second is that there is perfect knowledge about how these developments are going to affect well-being. These two assumptions are clearly at odds with our real-world situation. Debates on eco-environmental perspectives are dominated by ignorance and uncertainty about future interactions between the two spheres, and by a lack of consensus about the very definition of the objective function.

Let's briefly develop the first point. The future is fundamentally uncertain. Uncertainty takes many forms, some of them amenable to probability computation, while many others are much more radical. This affects not only the parameters of any models that one may try to use to project eco-environmental interactions, but also the structure of the models themselves, the measurement of current stocks and even the list of the natural assets for which current and future stocks need to be taken into account. Most of the debate concerning long-term environmental change reflects different beliefs about future eco-environmental scenarios. There is no reason why sustainability measurement should escape such difficulties.

Some solutions might be considered for this problem. One is to do what all prospectivists do when they want to emphasize the uncertain nature of future trends, i.e., work with scenarios or provide confidence intervals. One could also consider submitting indices to some form of "stress test," i.e., recompute them under assumptions of external shocks on asset values. This could include sudden upward adjustments in the value of environmental assets, but also drastic reductions in the value of some other items—such as produced capital and human capital. Such modes of presentation could be explored and eventually adopted.

But this could still be insufficient or difficult to present in a convenient way. Questions such as climate change require a specific consideration which drives us back to the distinction between weak and strong sustainability. The point is not that aggregate indices are by nature unable to account for situations of strong nonsustainability. The point is that we would be able to do so only by adopting extreme valuations of critical environmental assets, and that we are not that well equipped to quantify precisely what these extreme valuations should be. In such cases, and *a fortiori* for items for which we do not even have a single guestimate of a monetary value, a separate physical accounting is unavoidable.

The problem then is to present such an index in a compelling way. Monetary indices have the advantage of using units that speak to everyone. In addition, they can be related to other monetary quantities: this is what we do when we compute extended savings rates, and the orders of magnitude of such savings rates can be understood easily. On the other hand, a tonnage of CO_2 emissions is not a very informative number if we do not have some reference for how many tons can be emitted each year without severe consequences for the climate. Other physical indicators have been advocated by climate specialists, including "CO_2 radiative forcing," measuring the effect of CO_2 on the Earth's energy imbalance and measuring the regression of permanent ice. But it is difficult for non-experts to take such indicators on board. It is essential to find more suggestive ways to highlight such figures if we want the indicator to have an impact on the debate. One of the major successes of the EF has been its ability to express pressure on the environment in an easily understandable unit. The EF indicator has limits that make it problematic to many observers. But, given the objective of limiting climate change, the general idea of using the footprint as a generic unit for the different forms of pressure that mankind exerts on Earth's regenerative capacity is an option. A metric like this is used, for instance, with the more focused concept of the Carbon Footprint or the kindred concept of the CO_2 budget.

Uncertainty Is Also Normative

In addition to raising technological issues, measuring sustainability with a single index number would confront us with severe normative questions. The point is that there can be as many indices of sustainability as there are normative definitions of *what* we want to sustain. In standard national accounting practice, the normative issue of defining preferences is generally avoided through the assumption that observed prices reveal the true preferences of people. No explicit normative choice is therefore to be made by the statistician. But as soon as we recognize that market prices cannot be trusted, alternative imputed prices must be computed, whose values will strongly depend upon normative choices.

Can we solve this normative problem? One could attempt to solve it empirically by trying to infer the definition of well-being from current observations of how people value environmental factors compared to economic ones, using contingent valuations or direct measures of the impact of environmental amenities on indices of subjective well-being. But can the contingent evaluations and subjective measures established today in our specific eco-environmental setting be used to predict the valuations of future generations in eco-environmental settings that may have become very different? It could be argued that our descendants may become very sensitive to the relative scarcity of some environmental goods to which we pay little attention today because they are still relatively abundant, and that this requires that we immediately place a high value on these items just because we think that our descendants may wish to do so.

Another example of these normative issues is the question of determining how sustainability indices should aggregate individual preferences. This depends on how distributional considerations are taken into account in our measures of current well-being. For instance, if we consider that the headline indicator of current well-being must be the total disposable income of the bottom 80% of the population, or of the bottom 50%, rather than global disposable income, then sustainability indicators should be adapted to such an objective function. This would be in line with one of the other aspects of the Brundtland definition of sustainability that is often overlooked, i.e., its concern for the distribution of resources *within* as well as *between* generations. In a world where inequalities within countries naturally tend to increase, messages concerning sustainability will differ depending on the goal that we set ourselves. Specific attention to distributional issues may even suggest enlarging the list of capital goods that matter for sustainability: the "sustainability" of well-being for the bottom x% of the population may imply some specific investment in institutions that offer efficient help in protecting this population from poverty. In principle, the theoretical framework based on extended wealth tells us how we could ideally put some value on this kind of "institutional" investment. But, needless to say, the prospect of actually being able to do this is still more remote than for other assets.

An Additional Source of Complexity: The Global Dimension

A global context poses additional problems for sustainability indicators. Advocates of the ANS argue that sustainability problems generally concentrate in poor resource-exporting countries even if it is in developed countries that the resources are ultimately consumed. The argument is that, if markets work properly, the pressure that developed countries exert on other countries' resources is already reflected in the prices that they pay for importing these resources. If, despite the cost of their imports, the developed countries can still maintain a positive ANS, this means that they invest enough to compensate for their consumption of natural resources. It is then the responsibility of exporting countries to reinvest the income from their exports in sufficient quantities if they also want to be on a sustainable path.

Yet this logic holds true only under the assumption of efficient markets. If markets are not efficient and if the natural resource is underpriced, then importing countries benefit from an implicit subsidy while the exporting ones are effectively taxed. This means that the actual sustainability of developed countries is overestimated, while that of the developing countries is underestimated. And this problem will be all the more crucial when there are no markets at all, or in the presence of strong externalities.

To illustrate this issue, let's imagine a very simple two-country setting, where both countries produce and consume with external effects on the stock of a natural resource that is a global public good with free access. Country 2 uses a clean technology that has no impact on the natural resource, while country 1 uses a "dirty" one that leads to a depreciation of the resource. Let's push the asymmetry further by assuming that it is only country 2 that is affected by the degradation of the environmental good. Country 1 is completely indifferent to the level of degradation of this environmental good, for instance because its geographical characteristics fully protect it from the consequences.

In such a setting, it is natural to redefine countries 1 and 2 as being respectively "the polluter" and "the polluted." In this setting, there are two ways to consider sustainability. One is to compute changes in extended wealth for each country using country-specific accounting prices for the natural resource. The idea is that the environmental good is a common asset, but valued differently by each country, because they are not concerned in the same way by its degradation. In this example, the accounting price for the polluter will be zero, because we have assumed that it is not impacted at all by environmental changes, which implies that it attributes no value at all to the environmental asset. On the other hand, the polluted country will attribute a positive value to the asset. The message conveyed using this extended wealth concept is that the polluter is on a sustainable path, while the polluted is not.

From a certain point of view, it is correct to say that the polluter is not confronted by the prospect of a decline in well-being, in contrast to the polluted. But from another viewpoint, the message is clearly misleading. There is nothing the polluted can do to restore its sustainability. It is only a change in the polluter's technology that could help restore the polluted country's sustainability. We are in need of indices that would convey such a message. The popularity of footprint indicators stems precisely from the fact that, whatever their other limitations, they are able to send such messages to policymakers and public opinion. This is one more argument in favor of an eclectic approach that mixes points of views. An approach centered on national sustainabilities may be relevant for some dimensions of sustainability, but not for others. Global warming is a typical example of the latter case, as the prospective consequences of climate change are distributed very unevenly, without necessarily correlating with a country's CO_2 emissions.

Conclusion

To sum up, what have we learned, and what can we conclude? This trip through the world of sustainability indicators has been a bit lengthy, and we have not been able to avoid technicalities completely. A wide variety of indicators are already available and we have analyzed the reasons why a comprehensive assessment of sustainability is difficult to establish in a fully consensual way. Assessing sustainability requires many assumptions and normative choices, and it is further complicated by the existence of interactions between the socio-economic and environmental models followed by the different nations. The issue is indeed complex, more complex than the already complicated issue of measuring current well-being or performance. But we shall nevertheless try to articulate a limited set of recommendations, which we shall also try to keep as pragmatic as possible.

Recommendation 1: Sustainability assessment requires a well-identified sub-dashboard of the global dashboard to be recommended by the Commission.

The question of sustainability is complementary to the question of current well-being or economic performance, and must be examined separately. This recommendation to separate the two issues might look trivial. Yet it deserves emphasis, because some approaches fail to adopt this principle, leading to confusing messages. The confusion reaches a peak when one tries to combine these two dimensions into a single indicator. This criticism applies not only to composite indices, but also to the notion of Green GDP. To take an analogy, when driving a car, a meter that weighed up in one single value the current speed of the vehicle and the remaining level of gasoline would not be of any help to the driver. Both pieces of information are critical and need to be displayed in distinct, clearly visible areas of the dashboard.

Recommendation 2: The distinctive feature of all components of this sub-dashboard should be to inform about variations of those "stocks" that underpin human well-being.

In order to measure sustainability, what we need are indicators that tell us the sign of the change in the quantities of the different factors that matter for future well-being. Putting the sustainability issue in these terms compels recognition that sustainability requires the simultaneous preservation or increase in several "stocks": quantities and qualities not only of natural resources but also of human, social and physical capital. Any approach that focuses on only a part of these items does not offer a comprehensive view of sustainability.

Speaking in such terms also avoids many of the misconceptions about the messages sent by traditional national accounts indicators. For instance, a frequent criticism of GDP is that it classifies ecological catastrophes as blessings for the economy, because of the additional economic activity generated by repairs. The stock approach to sustainability clearly avoids this ambiguity. Catastrophes will be recorded as a form of depreciation of natural or physical capital. Any resulting increase in economic activity would have a positive value only insofar as it helps to restore the initial level of the capital stock.

Recommendation 3: A monetary index of sustainability has its place in such a dashboard, but under the current state of the art, it should remain essentially focused on economic aspects of sustainability.
The stock approach to sustainability can in turn be broken down into two versions. One version would just look at variations in each stock separately with a view to doing whatever is necessary to keep it from declining or at least to keep it above some critical threshold beyond which further reductions would be highly detrimental to future well-being. Or one could attempt to summarize all stock variations in synthetic figures.

This second track is the one followed by so-called extended wealth or adjusted savings approaches, which share the idea of converting all these assets into a monetary equivalent. We have discussed the potential of such an approach, but also its limitations. In certain conditions, it allows us to anticipate many forms of non-sustainability, but the requirements for such a capacity are extremely high. This is because the aggregation required by this approach cannot be based on market values: market prices are non-existent for quite a large number of the assets that matter for future well-being. Even when they are available, there is no guarantee that they adequately reflect how these different assets will matter for future well-being. In the absence of such price messages, we have to turn to imputations, which raises both normative and informational difficulties.

All this suggests staying with a more modest approach, i.e., focusing the monetary aggregation on items for which reasonable valuation techniques exist, such as physical capital, human capital and natural resources that are traded in markets. This more or less corresponds to the hard part of "adjusted net savings" as computed by the World Bank and further developed by several authors. "Greening" this index more intensively is of course a relevant objective, and we can keep it on the agenda but we know that the analytical apparatus for doing so is a complex one: large-scale projection models of interactions between the environment and the economy, projecting changes in the relative scarcities of corresponding assets and their impact on relative accounting prices, and allowing also a proper treatment of uncertainties or potential irreversibilities that affect these interactions. Meanwhile, we must focus this indicator essentially on what it does relatively well, i.e., the assessment of the "economic" component of sustainability, that is, the assessment of whether or not countries overconsume their economic wealth.

Recommendation 4: The environmental aspects of sustainability deserve a separate follow-up based on a well-chosen set of physical indicators.
As far as environmental sustainability is concerned, the limitations of monetary approaches do not mean that efforts to monetize

damages to the environment are no longer needed: it is well known that fully opposing any kind of monetization often leads to policies that act as if environmental goods had no value at all. The point is that we are far from being able to construct monetary values for environmental goods that at the macro level can be reasonably compared to market prices of other capital assets. Given our state of ignorance, the precautionary principle legitimates a separate follow-up of these environmental goods.

Another reason for a separate treatment is that these environmental issues often pertain to global public goods, such as the case of the climate. In such cases, the problem with the standard extended wealth approach is that it essentially focuses on country-specific sustainabilities. With global public goods, what is involved is more the contributions by the different countries to global unsustainabilities.

The EF could have been an option for this kind of follow-up. In particular, in contrast to net adjusted savings, it essentially focuses on contributions to global non-sustainability, with the message that the main responsibility lies with the developed countries. Yet the group has taken note of its limitations, and in particular that it is far from being a pure physical indicator of pressure on the environment: it retains some aggregation rules that may be problematic. In fact, much of the information that it conveys about national contributions to non-sustainability is imbedded in a simpler indicator, the Carbon Footprint, which is therefore one good candidate for monitoring humanity's pressure on the climate, among many indicators proposed by climatologists that are shortly reviewed in the technical report.

For other aspects of environmental sustainability, such as air quality, water quality, biodiversity and so on, one can again borrow from these large eclectic dashboards. Just to note a few of the indicators already incorporated in such dashboards, we could mention smog-forming pollutant emissions, nutrient loading to water bodies, the abundance of key specified natural species, rates of conversion of natural habitats to other uses, the proportion of fish catches beyond safe biological limits and many others. Today, at this stage of the debate, economists do not have any particular qualification for suggesting what the right choices are. This is why we will not propose any closed list of these indicators here.

In short, our pragmatic compromise is to suggest a small dashboard, firmly rooted in the logic of the "stock" approach to sustainability, which would combine:

- An indicator more or less derived from the extended wealth approach, "greened" as far as possible on the basis of currently available knowledge, but whose main function, however, would be to send warning messages concerning "economic" non-sustainability. This economic non-sustainability could be due to low savings or low investment in education, or to insufficient reinvestment of income generated by the extraction of fossil resources (for countries that strongly rely on this source of income).
- A set of well-chosen *physical* indicators, which would focus on dimensions of environmental sustainability that are either already important or could become so in the future, and that remain difficult to capture in monetary terms.

This scenario has several points of convergence with conclusions reached by other reports recently devoted to the topic, such as the recent OECD/Eurostat/UNECE report on sustainability measurement, whose conclusions were released in 2008, or the more recent report by the French Economic, Social and Environmental Council released in 2009. The first one, in particular, strongly advocates the stock-based approach to sustainability and proposes a small dashboard clearly separating assets that can be monetarized in a reasonable way and other assets for which separate physical measures are necessary. The second one warns against limits of the EF and, as far as climatic change is concerned, argues in favor of the Carbon Footprint index. Such points of convergence are reassuring: they suggest that from a relatively confused situation we are steadily moving towards a more consensual framework for the understanding of sustainability issues (see the box below).[9]

Physical and Other Non-Monetary Indicators: Which Ones to Choose?

The Commission's general position has been to avoid formulating definitive turnkey proposals on any of the different issues it has raised. All proposals, rather, intend to stimulate further debate. This is all the more true in the domain of *physical* sustainability indicators where the expertise of specialists from other disciplines is crucial and was only indirectly represented in the Commission's composition.

Some suggestions can however be made, in connection with conclusions of some recent related reports.

In 2008, a OECD/UNECE/Eurostat working group produced a report on measuring sustainable development whose messages have several points in common with ours. It strongly advocates the stock-based approach to sustainability as the relevant way of structuring a micro dashboard of sustainability indicators gathering both stock and flow variables. It also suggests a line of demarcation between determinants of "economic" well-being (those that are the most directly amenable to monetary evaluation) and the determinants of "foundational" well-being, among which four couples of stock/flow environmental indicators devoted respectively to global warming, other forms of atmospheric pollution, quality of water and biodiversity. The details and positions of these indicators in the dashboard can be visualized in the following table.

Small set of sustainable development indicators proposed by the UNECE/OECD/Eurostat working group on sustainability measurement

Indicator domain	Stock indicator	Flow indicator
Foundational well-being	Health-adjusted life expectancy	Index of changes in age-specific mortality and morbidity
	Percentage of population with post-secondary education	Enrolment in post-secondary education
	Temperature deviations from normals	Greenhouse gas emissions
	Ground-level ozone and fine particulate concentrations	Smog-forming pollutant emissions
	Quality-adjusted water availability	Nutrient loadings to water bodies
	Fragmentation of natural habitats	Conversion of natural habitats to other uses
Economic well-being	Real per-capita net foreign financial asset holdings	Real per-capita investment in foreign financial assets
	Real per-capita produced capital	Real per-capita net investment in produced capital
	Real per-capita human capital	Real per-capita net investment in human capital
	Real per-capita natural capital	Real per-capita net depletion of natural capital
	Reserves of energy resources	Depletion of energy resources
	Reserves of mineral resources	Depletion of mineral resources
	Timber resource stocks	Depletion of timber resources
	Marine resource stocks	Depletion of marine resources

Source: UNECE/OECD/Eurostat (2008).

(*Continued*)

(Continued)

More recently, the French Economic, Social and Environmental Council (CESE) has produced a report whose initial aim was the assessment of the Ecological Footprint but that has more widely explored the different tracks available for quantifying sustainability. It has the same messages as the current report concerning the limits of this EF index, and the fact that most of the relevant information that it conveys is more directly and more neatly reflected in one of its subcomponents, the Carbon Footprint. As a consequence, it strongly advocates in favor of this index. Compared to Global GHG emissions suggested in the OECD/UNECE/Eurostat Dashboard presented above, the Carbon Footprint has the advantage of being expressed in this "footprint" unit that is intuitively so appealing and that has made the success of the EF. In addition to this, this CESE report has suggested emphasizing the other physical indicators already present in large international dashboards such as the one elaborated for the European Union Strategy for Sustainable Development. Some of them are those already quoted in the OECD/UNECE/Eurostat Dashboard.

As far as climate change is concerned, some other indicators can be considered. Direct observation of mean temperature is one possibility but not the best suited, because it has a tendency to run behind the main components of climate change and because there can always be disagreements about the causes of temperature rises, hence about their permanent or transient character. Consequently, climatologists prefer to make use of a thermodynamic concept, the CO_2 radiative forcing, that measures the earth energy imbalance created by the action of CO_2 as a greenhouse gas.

Alternatively, it is possible to directly use a notion of a CO_2 remaining budget: according to climatologists, there is an upper limit of 0.75 trillion tonnes of carbon that might be discharged in the atsmosphere if the risk of temperatures exceeding 2° Celsius above pre-industrial levels is limited to one-in-four, this upperbound at 2°C being largely accepted among climate experts as a "tipping point" opening the door to unstoppable feedback effects (methane from melting permafrost, CO_2 and methane from decaying tropical forests, all sorts of green-

(Continued)

house gases released by saturated warming oceans, etc. . . .). Of this 0.75 total budget, emissions to 2008 have already consumed circa 0.5. Hence the importance of monitoring this remaining CO_2 budget. The attractiveness of this indicator is to be strongly consistent with the stock-based approach to sustainability. It can be also rephrased in the very expressive terms of a countdown index, i.e., the time that remains until exhaustion of this stock, under the assumption of emissions remaining on their current trend. This kind of representation is often used for other forms of exhaustible resources.

Still other indirect indicators of global warming are the regression of permanent ice or the oceanic pH. The regression of permanent ice has the advantage of being an advanced one and to be directly related to manifest effects. The oceanic pH increases with the amount of CO_2 that is naturally pumped into the oceans. A consequence of this increase is a decrease in the quantity of phytoplankton, which is itself a carbon sink no less important than the forests. One may therefore say that the physical sink (sea water dissolving atmospheric CO_2) destroys the biological one. This is the reason why the oceanic pH appears to be another good tentative indicator of climate change, pointing to one of the most vicious feedback effects. Among criteria for choosing between all the indicators, two are of particular importance. One is their appropriability by the public, the other is the capacity of declining them at national or even subnational levels: in this respect, the Carbon Footprint has quite a lot of advantages.

As far as biodiversity is concerned, the issue is currently under review by the TEEB ("the economics of the environment and biodiversity") group working at the initiative of the European Union and it has been also recently addressed by a report by the French *Conseil d'Analyse Stratégique*, in this case with the idea of pushing as far as possible the monetization of this dimension. The reason for this search of monetary equivalent is essentially that it may foster incorporation of this dimension in investment choices: many public decisions such as building a new motorway imply some potential biodiversity loss through fragmentation of natural habitats. But the report also provides a very detailed and technical review of available

(*Continued*)

(Continued)

physical measures of biodiversity, to which the reader is referred for further information.

At last, moving away from environmental preoccupations, but still on the "non-monetary" side, one important issue is the issue of social capital and "institutional assets" that we transmit to future generations. One will have noticed that the UNECE/OECD/Eurostat Dashboard presented above did not propose any indicator of this kind, not because the question is not relevant, but mainly because of lack of consensus about the way to measure it. Subgroup 3 was not in a position to explore this question further, but efforts along this direction remain undoubtedly necessary.

A subsidiary question concerns a user's guide to such a dashboard. A warning should be given that no limited set of figures can pretend to forecast the sustainable or unsustainable character of a highly complex system with certainty. The purpose is, rather, to have a set of indicators that give an "alert" to situations that pose a high risk of non-sustainability. Whatever we do, however, dashboards and indices are only one part of the story. Most of the efforts involved in assessing sustainability focus on increasing our knowledge about how the economy and the environment interact now and are likely to interact in the future.

NOTES

1. Evidence and references in support of the claims presented in this Summary are presented in a companion technical report.

2. Evidence and references in support of the claims presented in this Summary are presented in a companion technical report.

3. See, for example, the Taxonomy developed by the OECD in the context of the "Global Project on Measuring the Progress of Societies" (www.oecd.org/progress/taxonomy).

4. Note however that there is ongoing research to measure socio-economic inequalities to health in a standard way. See for example the European Union Working Group in Socio-economic Inequalities to Health.

5. Environmental insecurity is not developed here since this issue is already considered above.

6. While insecurity is dealt with as an objective factor shaping quality of life, it can also be considered as a cross-cutting issue because of the large variety of risks the individuals are exposed to. The placement of insecurity among the objective factors has been debated at some length and is conventional.

7. Evidence and references in support of the claims presented in this Summary are presented in a companion technical report.

8. As for local pollution damages, these are difficult to estimate without location-specific data. Nevertheless, an augmented version of ANS for local pollution is also provided by taking into account health damage due to urban air pollution (particulate matter PM10).

9. Some other points of convergence can be found in reactions by the European Environmental Agency to the first draft of this Commission's summary report.